JACQUES LACAN

D0143922

Jacques Lacan is one of the most challenging and controversial of contemporary thinkers, as well as the most influential psychoanalyst since Freud. Lacanian theory has reached far beyond the consulting room to engage with such diverse disciplines as literature, film, gender and social theory. This book covers the full extent of Lacan's career and provides an accessible guide to Lacanian concepts and his writing on:

- the imaginary and the symbolic
- the Oedipus complex and the meaning of the phallus
- the subject and the unconscious
- the real
- sexual difference.

Locating Lacan's work in the context of contemporary French thought and the history of psychoanalysis, Sean Homer's *Jacques Lacan* is the ideal introduction to this influential theorist.

Sean Homer is Senior Lecturer in Media Studies at City College, Greece. He is the author of *Fredric Jameson* (1998) and co-editor (with Douglas Kellner) of *Fredric Jameson: A Critical Reader* (2004).

ROUTLEDGE CRITICAL THINKERS

Series Editor: Robert Eaglestone, Royal Holloway, University of London

Routledge Critical Thinkers is a series of accessible introductions to key figures in contemporary critical thought.

With a unique focus on historical and intellectual contexts, each volume examines a key theorist's:

- significance
- motivation
- key ideas and their sources
- impact on other thinkers

Concluding with extensively annotated guides to further reading, *Routledge Critical Thinkers* are the student's passport to today's most exciting critical thought.

Already available:

For further details on this series, see www.literature.routledge.com/literature

JACQUES LACAN

Sean Homer

Routledge
Taylor & Francis Group

LONDON AND NEW YORK

First published 2005
by Routledge
2 Park Square, Milton Park, Abingdon, Oxon OX14 4RN

Simultaneously published in the USA and Canada
by Routledge
711 Third Avenue, New York, NY 10017

Routledge is an imprint of the Taylor & Francis Group, an informa business

© 2005 Sean Homer

Typeset in Perpetua by
Florence Production Ltd, Stoodleigh, Devon
Printed and bound in Great Britain by
TJ International Ltd, Padstow, Cornwall

British Library Cataloguing in Publication Data
A catalogue record for this book is available from the
British Library

Library of Congress Cataloging in Publication Data
A catalog record for this book has been requested

ISBN10: 0–415–25616–X (hbk)
ISBN10: 0–415–25617–8 (pbk)

ISBN13: 978–0–415–25616–2 (hbk)
ISBN13: 978–0–415–25617–9 (pbk)

CONTENTS

SERIES EDITOR'S PREFACE

The books in this series offer introductions to major critical thinkers who have influenced literary studies and the humanities. The *Routledge Critical Thinkers* series provides the books you can turn to first when a new name or concept appears in your studies.

Each book will equip you to approach a key thinker's original texts by explaining her or his key ideas, putting them into context and, perhaps most importantly, showing you why this thinker is considered to be significant. The emphasis is on concise, clearly written guides which do not presuppose a specialist knowledge. Although the focus is on particular figures, the series stresses that no critical thinker ever existed in a vacuum but, instead, emerged from a broader intellectual, cultural and social history. Finally, these books will act as a bridge between you and the thinker's original texts: not replacing them but rather complementing what she or he wrote.

These books are necessary for a number of reasons. In his 1997 autobiography, *Not Entitled*, the literary critic Frank Kermode wrote of a time in the 1960s:

> On beautiful summer lawns, young people lay together all night, recovering from their daytime exertions and listening to a troupe of Balinese musicians. Under their blankets or their sleeping bags, they would chat drowsily about the

gurus of the time. ... What they repeated was largely hearsay; hence my
lunchtime suggestion, quite impromptu, for a series of short, very cheap books
offering authoritative but intelligible introductions to such figures.

There is still a need for 'authoritative and intelligible introductions'.
But this series reflects a different world from the 1960s. New thinkers
have emerged and the reputations of others have risen and fallen, as
new research has developed. New methodologies and challenging ideas
have spread through arts and humanities. The study of literature is no
longer – if it ever was – simply the study and evaluation of poems,
novels and plays. It is also the study of the ideas, issues, and difficulties
which arise in any literary text and in its interpretation. Other arts and
humanities subjects have changed in analogous ways.

With these changes, new problems have emerged. The ideas and
issues behind these radical changes in the humanities are often
presented without reference to wider contexts or as theories which
you can simply 'add on' to the texts you read. Certainly, there's
nothing wrong with picking out selected ideas or using what comes
to hand – indeed, some thinkers have argued that this is, in fact, all
we can do. However, it is sometimes forgotten that each new idea
comes from the pattern and development of somebody's thought and
it is important to study the range and context of their ideas. Against
theories 'floating in space', the *Routledge Critical Thinkers* series places
key thinkers and their ideas firmly back in their contexts.

More than this, these books reflect the need to go back to the
thinker's own texts and ideas. Every interpretation of an idea, even
the most seemingly innocent one, offers its own 'spin', implicitly or
explicitly. To read only books on a thinker, rather than texts by that
thinker, is to deny yourself a chance of making up your own mind.
Sometimes, what makes a significant figure's work hard to approach is
not so much its style or content as the feeling of not knowing where
to start. The purpose of these books is to give you a 'way in' by offering
an accessible overview of these thinkers' ideas and works and by
guiding your further reading, starting with each thinker's own texts.
To use a metaphor from the philosopher Ludwig Wittgenstein (1889–
1951), these books are ladders, to be thrown away after you have
climbed to the next level. Not only, then, do they equip you to
approach new ideas, but also they empower you, by leading you back

to the theorist's own texts and encouraging you to develop your own informed opinions.

Finally, these books are necessary because, just as intellectual needs have changed, the education systems around the world – the contexts in which introductory books are usually read – have changed radically, too. What was suitable for the minority higher education system of the 1960s is not suitable for the larger, wider, more diverse, high technology education systems of the twenty-first century. These changes call not just for new, up-to-date, introductions but new methods of presentation. The presentational aspects of *Routledge Critical Thinkers* have been developed with today's students in mind.

Each book in the series has a similar structure. They begin with a section offering an overview of the life and ideas of each thinker and explain why she or he is important. The central section of each book discusses the thinker's key ideas, their context, evolution and reception. Each book concludes with a survey of the thinker's impact, outlining how their ideas have been taken up and developed by others. In addition, there is a detailed final section suggesting and describing books for further reading. This is not a 'tacked-on' section but an integral part of each volume. In the first part of this section you will find brief descriptions of the thinker's key works: following this, information on the most useful critical works and, in some cases, on relevant websites. This section will guide you in your reading, enabling you to follow your interests and develop your own projects. Throughout each book, references are given in what is known as the Harvard system (the author and the date of a work cited are given in the text and you can look up the full details in the bibliography at the back). This offers a lot of information in very little space.

The thinkers in the series are 'critical' for three reasons. First, they are examined in the light of subjects which involve criticism: principally literary studies or English and cultural studies, but also other disciplines which rely on the criticism of books, ideas, theories and unquestioned assumptions. Second, they are critical because studying their work will provide you with a 'tool kit' for your own informed critical reading and thought, which will make you critical. Third, these thinkers are critical because they are crucially important: they deal with ideas and questions which can overturn conventional understandings of the world, of texts, of everything we take for granted, leaving us with a deeper understanding of what we already knew and with new ideas.

No introduction can tell you everything. However, by offering a way into critical thinking, this series hopes to begin to engage you in an activity which is productive, constructive and potentially life-changing.

ACKNOWLEDGEMENTS

I would like to thank Bob Eaglestone and Liz Thompson for their patience and encouragement during the writing of this book. I would also like to thank Eugenie Georgaca for her invaluable criticism and advice.

WHY LACAN?

Jacques Lacan (1901–81) is arguably the most important psychoanalyst since Sigmund Freud (1856–1939), the originator and founding father of psychoanalysis. Deeply controversial, Lacan's work has transformed psychoanalysis, both as a theory of the unconscious mind and as a clinical practice. Over 50 per cent of the world's analysts now employ Lacanian methods. At the same time, Lacan's influence beyond the confines of the consulting room is unsurpassed among modern psychoanalytic thinkers. Lacanian thought now pervades the disciplines of literary and film studies, women's studies and social theory and is applied to such diverse fields as education, legal studies and international relations. For a student of the humanities and the social sciences today it is almost impossible not to engage with the ideas of Lacan at some level; if not first hand, then through a thinker he has influenced (or enraged, as we shall see). Works such as Laura Mulvey's 'Visual Pleasure and Narrative Cinema' (1975) and Jacqueline Rose's *Sexuality in the Field of Vision* (1986); Shoshana Felman's *Literature and Psychoanalysis, The Question of Reading: Otherwise* (1982) and Peter Brooks's *Reading for the Plot* (1992); or Louis Althusser's 'Freud and Lacan' (1984a [1964]) and Slavoj Žižek's *The Sublime Object of Ideology* (1989) are now considered classics in their respective fields.

From the perspective of literary studies, the discovery of Lacan in the mid-1970s, initially by feminist and Marxist literary critics, revitalized the rather moribund practice of psychoanalytic criticism and reinstated psychoanalysis at the cutting edge of critical theory. After much initial enthusiasm for Freudian and post-Freudian readings of literature (see Wright (1998) for an account of classical Freudian readings), psychoanalytic criticism had degenerated into the reductive practice of identifying Oedipal scenarios within texts and spotting phallic symbolism. Lacan's conception of the unconscious as structured like a language (see Chapter 4) and the relationship between the symbolic order and the subject (see Chapter 2) opened up a whole new way of understanding the play of unconscious desire in the text. The object of psychoanalytic criticism was no longer to hunt for phallic symbols or to explain Hamlet's hesitation to revenge his father's death by his repressed sexual desire for his mother (see Jones 1949) but to analyse the way unconscious desires manifest themselves in the text, through language. The focus of Lacanian criticism, therefore, is not upon the unconscious of the character or the author but upon the text itself and the relationship between text and reader. In film and women's studies the importation of these often strange and unfamiliar ideas from Paris has become almost synonymous with their establishment as university disciplines in the 1970s. Lacan's theory of the mirror phase and the formation of the ego (see Chapter 1) was taken by many film theorists as a model for the relationship between the film projected on the screen and how this affected the film viewer or cinematic spectator. Lacan's complex notion of how a subject comes to identify themselves as an 'I' in the social world was seen as a useful way of understanding how cinema spectators identify with images on the screen, beyond simply identifying positive and negative images (usually strong and positive images of men and passive or negative images of women). Similarly, Lacan's development of Freud's theory of sexual difference (see Chapter 6) opened up new areas of debate within women's and gender studies. In the 1970s women's studies tended to focus on the social aspects of gender, looking at social and familial influences on upbringing and identity. Lacanian psychoanalysis contributed to this work the crucial link of subjectivity to the unconscious and to language, as well as an understanding of sexual difference as constituted at an unconscious level. Finally, in the area of social theory and international relations figures such as the Slovenian Lacanian philosopher Slavoj Žižek had a tremendous impact on our appreciation of the unconscious processes and fantasies underlying social and national conflicts as well as racism, sexism and homophobia. I will return to and explain all of these terms and issues in the subsequent chapters, focusing in particular on the ways in which Lacanian ideas have been applied in the field of literary and cultural studies.

How can we summarize Lacan's project and his contribution to theory, then? Psychoanalysis originates with the work of Freud and remains rooted in his theories to this day, but every generation of analysts that came after Freud has sought to update and correct those theories, and to resolve the contradictions that he left behind. Lacan argued that through this process of continual revision psychoanalysis had lost sight of its original aims; that it had become conservative and reactionary. By playing down the more uncomfortable and disturbing aspects of the theory, especially the underlying presence of repressed, unconscious, desire in our mental lives, psychoanalysis had made itself respectable but it had lost its radical edge. In the early 1950s, therefore, Lacan famously declared the necessity of a 'return to Freud', that is to say, a return to the texts of Freud himself and to a close reading and understanding of those texts. For the next 26 years he would engage in this project of close reading, and in the process would reconstitute the theory of psychoanalysis.

To better understand this project and its significance, it is crucial that we briefly consider Lacan's work within the context of the development of psychoanalysis in France. I will discuss the contexts of Lacan's ideas in more detail in the following chapters, but it is important to gain an overview before we begin to look more closely at his work.

LACAN IN CONTEXT

Lacan grew up in a comfortable middle-class Catholic family in Montparnasse, Paris. He attended a prestigious Catholic school, the Collège Stanislas, where he was recognized as a very bright pupil, although not exceptional. Lacan did however excel in religious studies and Latin. While at school he developed a lifelong passion for philosophy and in particular the work of Baruch Spinoza (1632–77), which was overridingly concerned with the idea of God's existence. Spinoza was Jewish but was excommunicated as a heretic as a result of his work, and Christians also denounced him as an atheist. At school Lacan hung a diagram of the 'atheist' Spinoza's posthumously published *Ethics* on his bedroom wall – a clearly subversive act in light of his middle-class Catholic upbringing and a move often interpreted as an early indication of his attitude towards institutions and authority. After leaving school Lacan went on to study medicine and specialized in psychiatry with a particular interest in psychosis. He looked set to pursue a conventional career in psychiatry until in the early 1930s he had two crucial intellectual encounters. First, in 1930 he read an article in a Surrealist journal by a little-known painter Salvador Dali (1904–89) on 'Paranoia'. Second, in 1931 he began reading Freud. These two encounters were to propel Lacan on a lifelong engagement with – and transformation of – the field of psychoanalysis.

Psychoanalysis can be said to have begun with Freud and the publication in 1900 of *The Interpretation of Dreams* (see 1991a), and, shortly following this, with such texts as *The Psychopathology of Everyday Life* (1991b [1901]), *Jokes and their Relation to the Unconscious* and 'Three Essays on the Theory of Sexuality' (both 1905; see 1991c and d). In the 1920s, as interest grew in the newly emerging discipline of psychoanalysis, it was received with widely differing views in different countries. Initially, in North America and Britain both the psychiatric and psychological professions warmly embraced what Freud reportedly called the 'modern plague'. Freud was also extremely influential within modernist literature, and was promoted in particular by the novelist and critic Virginia Woolf (1882–1941) and the 'Bloomsbury Group', an intellectual circle in which Woolf figured large. In France, however, psychoanalysis was rejected on all fronts: scientific, medical, religious and political. As one critic notes, 'the French opposed psychoanalysis from so many directions that it is appropriate to speak of an "anti-psychoanalytic" culture' (Turkle 1992: 27). Indeed, even as late as the 1950s and early 1960s French psychiatry remained decidedly anti-psychoanalytic. In response to such opposition, the French psychoanalytic establishment – under the guidance of the Marie Bonaparte, an early disciple of Freud's and one of his closest associates – insisted that psychoanalysis was a science closely aligned to medicine. Bonaparte and her allies within the Société Psychanalytique de Paris (SPP) emphasized the biological and medical aspects of psychoanalysis and required anyone who wished to become an analyst to first undergo a medical training.

Surrealism, however, offered the young Lacan an alternative route to psychoanalysis and the crucial link to his clinical practice in psychiatry. The Surrealists fully embraced psychoanalysis and during his medical studies Lacan developed strong links with the movement. Surrealism was a literary and artistic movement that emerged after the First World War in Paris, its founding figure the writer and poet André Breton (1896–1966). Breton was familiar with Freud's work on dreams and developed a technique of 'spontaneous' writing to give free expression to unconscious thoughts and wishes. Similarly, Surrealist painters such as Dali attempted to paint the 'reality' of their dreams, which they saw as more 'real' than the prosaic reality of our everyday world. In 1932, and within this context, Lacan completed his doctoral thesis on *Paranoid Psychosis and Its Relations to the Personality*. Around the same time he entered analysis with Rudolph Loewenstein, the SPP's most famous training analyst (a recognized psychoanalyst who is qualified to train other analysts within the Society). There has always been something of a controversy around Lacan's analysis, with critics questioning how successful it was and whether or not he completed it. It is known to have been a very 'stormy' relationship and ended rancorously in 1938. What is clear is that Lacan spent six years in analysis – longer than was usual at this time – and that he remained in analysis until he was accepted as a training analyst. During this time, Lacan's links with the Surrealists developed further. He was a friend of André Breton and Salvador Dali, and was later to become the painter Pablo Picasso's (1881–1973) personal physician. He attended the first public readings of James Joyce's (1882–1941) *Ulysses* in 1921 and was a well-known figure in the cafés and bookshops of Paris's Left Bank. In 1933 Dali was to refer to Lacan's doctoral thesis in the first issue of the Surrealist review *Minotaure* and Lacan himself was to make many contributions to this and other Surrealist publications.

Lacan's doctoral thesis, then, was written in a largely anti-psychoanalytic culture and remained within established psychiatric categories and theories, but at the same time it drew on the alternative resources of the Surrealist movement. In the 1950s, when Lacan began a seminar, he would formulate his ideas in direct opposition to the biological emphasis of Marie Bonaparte and to 'Ego psychology'. Ego psychology developed in the United States in the years following the Second World War and focused on ways of strengthening the defence mechanisms of the conscious mind rather than the unconscious motivation of our actions, as in classical psychoanalysis. Rudolph Loewenstein,

Lacan's training analyst, had been one of the founding fathers of Ego psychology, having fled Nazi persecution in the 1940s. Lacan saw both as a betrayal of psychoanalysis. He was strongly opposed to the SPP's requirement that analysts undergo medical training and saw psychoanalysis as much more closely aligned to philosophy and the arts, and later to mathematics, than to medicine. From the outset Lacan's work was rooted on the one hand in clinical work but on the other in a broader cultural understanding of the unconscious and mental illness. Unlike Anglo-American psychiatry and psychology, the French tradition has always retained a more poetic or aesthetic element. This may be just one further reason why it became so pervasive in Humanities departments in the 1970s.

Influential though his work may eventually have been, from the start of his career Lacan set himself on a collision course with the psychoanalytic establishment. Indeed, from the time of his earliest publications, the name 'Lacan' has gone hand in hand with some of the most ferocious criticism you are likely to read. In an introduction which asks why Lacan is worth reading, and which seeks to give you some idea of his impact, it would be impossible not to look briefly at the question of his reputation, and not least at his reputation for difficulty.

CONTROVERSIAL REPUTATIONS

To say that Lacan is a controversial figure is an understatement in the extreme. Lacan was a very charismatic teacher and he is often described by biographers as flamboyant, charming and something of a dandy. He undoubtedly attracted, and continues to attract, intense loyalty from his followers and advocates. At the same time, he was extremely ambitious, arrogant and authoritarian (see Roudinesco 1999). As with all charismatic figures, Lacan attracts as much vitriol and attack as he does support. For example, Raymond Tallis's review of Elizabeth Roudinesco's biography of Lacan – Roudinesco is probably the foremost authority on the history of French psychoanalysis – in *The Times Higher Education Supplement* commenced thus:

> Future historians trying to account for the institutionalized fraud that goes under the name of 'Theory' will surely accord a central place to the influence of the French psychoanalyst Jacques Lacan. He is one of the fattest spiders at the heart of the web of muddled not-quite-thinkable-thoughts and evidence-

> free assertions of limitless scope, which practitioners of theorhoea have
> woven into their version of the humanities. Much of the dogma central to
> contemporary theory came from him.

(Tallis 1997: 20)

Tallis's review continues with the assertion that there is no empirical basis for Lacan's theory, followed by a remorseless attack on his personal life. The review finally draws to a close with the claim that this 'lunatic legacy' now only lives on in departments of English Literature, whose 'inmates' pretend to make sense of it:

> Lacanians may argue that the great edifice of the *Écrits* is not undermined by
> revelations about his life: the Master's thoughts should be judged on their own
> merits. However, in the absence of any logical basis or empirical evidence, the
> authority of the thought has derived almost completely from the authority
> of the man.

(Tallis 1997: 20)

What is interesting in this review, from an analytic perspective, is the pathologization of both Lacan and his readers; in other words, the assertion by the reviewer Raymond Tallis that both Lacan as an analyst and we as students and readers of Lacan are mentally ill in some way if we pretend (for, of course, there is no sense to be made of it) to understand what we are talking about. We are like mental patients locked in an asylum, inflicting our paranoid delusions on others. As a rhetorical (persuasive) strategy this is very effective because it pre-supposes that the writer of the piece has a firm grip on reality and everything that he says and does is rational, logical and evidence-based. It effectively places the reviewer in a position of superiority to that of the sadly deluded individuals who read Lacan.

This review raises two important points that need to be addressed if we are to appreciate the contribution that psychoanalysis and Lacan himself have made to our understanding of cultural texts. First, from its inception psychoanalysis has consistently been attacked as having no firm basis in reality and therefore for being unverifiable. Such attacks also generally assert that the lives of the analysts can be used to discredit their theories. Second, it is precisely the assumptions underlying this review that are questioned by psychoanalysis: the assumption that our theories and views of the world are detached from our position as subjects within it. In other words, psychoanalysis questions the fact that we are purely rational objective beings and that our actions are all logically and rationally driven. Psychoanalysis is not concerned with what is logical, what is rational and what is conscious; on the contrary, it is concerned with what is illogical, irrational and unconscious. Psychoanalysis looks at those aspects of thinking and behaviour for which we cannot rationally or consciously account. This book is not the place to discuss the efficacy of psychoanalysis and whether or not one can empirically prove or disprove the theory. What I will do, however, is take Lacan's theory on its 'own merits' and judge it within its own context, that is to say, in the context of the work of Freud, the history of psychoanalysis and of French intellectual life. In doing so I will suggest that, while Lacan may often be contradictory and elusive, and even infuriating to some, there is much to be gained from a careful reading and rereading of his texts. Lacan, like Freud before him, has transformed the way we think about ourselves and our place within the social world.

READING LACAN

When you pick up a copy of Freud for the first time, however unusual and perplexing you may find the ideas contained within the text, it is difficult to remain immune to the pleasure of the writing itself. Reading Freud, especially the case studies and the speculative works on art, society and religion, is like reading a good detective novel. Indeed, this was one of Freud's favourite literary genres and analogies for analysis. Even if you are not convinced by the arguments, you remain gripped by the story Freud tells. With Lacan the situation is very different. As the angry critics have already announced, when you pick up Lacan for the first time you will find a text that is dense, convoluted, elliptical and seemingly impenetrable, even by the standards of contemporary literary and cultural theory. Why is this?

Lacanian ideas first entered the humanities departments of British universities through the simultaneous publication of two texts: Alan Sheridan's translations of *Écrits: A Selection* and *The Four Fundamental Concepts of Psycho-Analysis*, both published in the UK in 1977. For many students these texts represent their first introduction to Lacan, and papers from *Écrits*, such as 'The Mirror Stage' and 'The Signification of the Phallus', remain some of the most frequently reproduced and anthologized of Lacan's writings. Both of these texts, however, present particular difficulties for reading Lacan.

Lacan was first and foremost a clinician and then a teacher. He was not an academic or a writer and he remained deeply suspicious of the university and of what he called the discourse of the university. He also remained suspicious of publishing his work and, towards the end of his career, in seminar XX, he would refer to the *Écrits* as a *poubellication*, a pun that combines *poubelle* (a waste bin) and *publication* (publication). In 1953 Lacan began a fortnightly public seminar at Hôpital Sainte-Anne, the psychiatric hospital where he worked (for the previous two years he had given private weekly lectures in the apartment of Sylvia Bataille, then the wife of the philosopher and writer George Bataille (1897–1962) and shortly to become Lacan's second wife). The seminar would continue for the next 26 years. Each year he would take a text or concept from Freud and devote the seminar to the study of that text or idea. Under the general editorship of Jacques Alain-Miller many of these seminars have now been reconstructed from notes and transcripts made by his former students, and a steadily increasing number have been translated (see the 'Further Reading' section for details). The articles collected in *Écrits*, the English selection of which is approximately a third of the French edition, often represent a summary or conclusion of the ideas that Lacan had developed over a whole year's seminar. The *Écrits*, therefore, should not be read as an introduction to the work of Lacan so much as a very condensed presentation of his ideas for those already initiated into them. For those reading Lacan for the first time it is often better to approach him through the early seminars, of which volumes I, II, III and VII are all now widely available. In saying this, one should also be aware that Lacan's theory, as with that of any innovative thinker, was not static, but changed and developed throughout his life. These early seminars represent the first, 'structuralist', phase of Lacan's career (see Chapter 2) and much of the most interesting work that is now being done in the field of Lacanian studies draws on his later work from the 1960s and 1970s. This change in our appreciation of Lacan is reflected in the emphasis placed on the later work in the latter half of this book. A further difficulty with reading Lacan is that, once he had introduced a concept such as the object *a*, the Other, the real or the phallus, he would retain the term in his writing but gradually change its meaning. Thus Lacan's concepts acquired different levels of meaning as his thinking developed but he never abandoned their original definition. For this reason it is not possible to give a simple definition of Lacanian terms as they always function differently according to each of Lacan's three orders – the imaginary, the symbolic and the real – and in the different phases of his teaching.

The second text translated in 1977 presents us with a slightly different set of issues. *The Four Fundamental Concepts of Psycho-Analysis* is in fact a transcription of Lacan's eleventh seminar series. This is one of Lacan's most important seminars and central to his work; it is also an extremely dense and difficult text to read. Again, there are specific reasons for this. The seminar was given in 1964 and marked a pivotal moment in Lacan's career and the development of his thought. In 1963 he had finally broken with the psychoanalytic establishment and founded his own school, seminar XI was in a sense the first public statement of his new direction. In 1953 a group of analysts, including Lacan, had left the Société Psychanalytique de Paris (SPP) over the issue of training and the medicalization of psychoanalysis and went on to form the Société Française de Psychanalyse (SFP). What these analysts did not realize at the time was that by leaving the 'official' society they were also leaving the International Psycho-Analytical Association (IPA). For the next ten years the SFP held negotiations with the IPA to gain recognition of their new society, without which they could not call themselves psychoanalysts and practise. In 1963 the IPA finally rejected the SFP request for readmission and Lacan, among others, was expelled from the IPA. In the same year the SFP split and Lacan founded his own school of psychoanalysis, the École Freudienne de Paris (EFP). As a result of his break with the SFP Lacan was forced to move his seminar from Sainte-Anne psychiatric hospital and, at the invitation of the Marxist philosopher Louis Althusser (1918–90), who in that year published an important essay on Freud and Lacan, he transferred the seminar to the École Normale Supérieure (ENS). The ENS is one of the elite institutions of the French educational system and it brought Lacan a whole new audience for his work. This was also a time, partly as a result of Althusser's article, when psychoanalysis began to spread and become more accepted among Parisian intellectuals and cultural life. The move, therefore, raised a number of theoretical problems for Lacan. For the previous ten years his seminar had been devoted to the close reading and explication of Freud and had been directed at clinicians and practitioners of psychoanalysis. Now he was addressing an audience that included students, political activists, philosophers, writers and cultural practitioners. How, then, was he to remain true to what he saw as the radicalism of psychoanalysis and at the same time teach it in a university system? In seminar XI, for the first time, Lacan moved away from an exposition of Freud's ideas to the development of his own conception of psychoanalysis. In other words, he began to develop what we would now recognize as a specifically Lacanian theory of the unconscious, of desire, of transference and of the drive (the four fundamental concepts of psychoanalysis). It was also at this time that the seminars began to get more complicated and enigmatic and, as the audience of his seminar grew, to over a thousand in his final year, so did the difficulty and complexity of many of his ideas and formulations. What needs to be kept in mind, therefore, when reading Lacan, is that the question of his style and the difficulty one encounters when reading his texts is not superfluous or simply gratuitous. To become an analyst one needs to go through a very long process of training, supervision and most importantly an analysis oneself. It is not something that can be taught in the lecture hall or seminar room. To a certain extent the difficulty of Lacan's style is precisely the self-conscious desire on his part to resist any easy assimilation and recuperation of his ideas. As Lacan himself puts it in seminar XX:

It is rather well known that those *Écrits* cannot be read easily. I can make a little autobiographical admission – that is exactly what I thought. I thought, perhaps it goes that far, I thought they were not meant to be read.

(1998 [1975]: 26)

A second aspect of this difficulty is related specifically to Lacan's object of study, that is to say, the unconscious itself.

According to Freud, the unconscious is a realm that does not know time or contradiction; it is a realm of repressed wishes and fantasies; and it is also a realm without syntax or grammar. In what sense then can we actually speak of unconscious wishes and desires? To speak of unconscious desire is to render it conscious and the unconscious, by definition, is that which is excluded from and cannot be recalled to consciousness. The unconscious, in other words, is that which is excluded from language. This paradoxical situation leaves the theorist and the analyst in something of a dilemma, for how can we discuss unconscious wishes and desires if we cannot put them into language? According to Freud, we can detect the workings of the unconscious through our anxieties and phobias, but we can also detect its effects through our dreams, jokes, slips of the tongue and works of art (see Thurschwell (2000) for an introduction to Freud). In other words, we can detect the workings of the unconscious at precisely those times when our conscious mind is least alert and active in *repressing* unwanted thoughts and desires. In his early work Lacan focused on this area of Freud's work and looked especially closely at those texts of Freud that dealt with questions of language and interpretation: *The Interpretation of Dreams* (1991a [1900]), *The Psychopathology of Everyday Life* (1991b [1901]) and *Jokes and their Relation to the Unconscious* (1991c [1905]). Lacan sought to tackle head on the paradox which always confronts psychoanalysis: if we can say that psychoanalysis is the discourse of the unconscious, or a discourse upon the unconscious, it is a discourse that rests upon something that is always beyond itself. His style is one of the ways in which he addresses the issue in the sense that his writing is an attempt to say what is essentially unsayable. In short, Lacan tries to articulate through the structure of language something that remains beyond language itself: the realm of unconscious desire. His writing is an attempt to force the reader to confront the limits of meaning and understanding and to acknowledge the profoundly disturbing prospect that behind all meaning lies non-meaning, and behind all sense lies non-sense. Thus, his prose 'often obeys the laws of the unconscious as they were formalised by Freud – it is full of puns, jokes, metaphors, irony and contradictions, and there are many similarities in its form to that of psychotic writing' (Benvenuto and Kennedy 1986: 12). One should never take Lacan too seriously: the puns, the wordplay and the elusive roundabout way of speaking are not superfluous but essential to an understanding of his work. This is a style of writing that is *performative* – that attempts to enact its meaning through its own presentation and syntax. As one critic suggests, Lacan wanted 'his communications to speak directly to the unconscious and believe[d] that word play, where causal links dissolve and associations abound, is the language which it understands' (Turkle 1992: 55). The next time you read Lacan and want to throw the book across the room, take a moment to sit back and consider what the text is doing to you. Think about how you feel at that moment and what effect the language has had upon you. As you begin to reflect upon this process the text will have achieved its purpose; the unconscious will be working.

THIS BOOK

The following section, 'Key Ideas', will introduce you to some of the most influential elements of Lacan's work, setting them in the contexts from which they emerged in order to help you understand what might at first seem a very strange and complex theory. The chapters will cover many key terms which run through psychoanalysis today, but my focus is on those ideas that have been widely used in literary and cultural studies, such as the imaginary, symbolic and the real, the mirror phase, the subject of the unconscious, the unconscious structured like a language, the phallus, fantasy, jouissance and sexual difference. I will not be looking at Lacan's graphs and 'mathemes' or his 'four discourses', as these ideas are not widely used within literary and cultural studies. Each chapter in this section will conclude with an example of how these ideas have been applied to literature, film or social theory. 'After Lacan' will extend these examples to discuss the different ways Lacan is currently being used in textual and film analysis as well as in political and social theory.

Lacanian psychoanalysis is not a static theory and has continued to evolve since Lacan's death. In 1980, one year before his death, Lacan dissolved his school, the EFP, and established the École de la Cause Freudienne (ECF). This school and its subsequent formations have been presided over by Lacan's son-in-law, Jacques-Alain Miller. As general editor of Lacan's seminar, and more importantly through his own seminar, Miller has begun to establish an 'orthodox' reading of Lacan, formalizing and systematizing his concepts. In this introduction I draw on Miller's work and that of his close associate, the North American academic and analyst Bruce Fink. Fink's introductions to Lacan very closely follow Miller's seminar and in this sense are easier to follow than Lacan's own writing. By attempting to make Lacan's ideas more consistent and presenting them as a coherent system, however, Miller's and Fink's texts lose the critical and abrasive edge that always makes Lacan so interesting to read. Therefore, I will juxtapose Fink's explications with Lacan's writing so that you can get a feel of his particular style. Full details of Fink's introductions and Lacan's own texts as well as a summary of other useful critical introductions are given in the 'Further Reading' section at the end of this book. You might notice throughout this book that dates in the references to Lacan's texts are very recent. I have quoted from recent translations of Lacan's works, all of which are listed in the 'Works Cited' section. I will mention the original dates of Lacan's works in the main body of the book, but the 'Further Reading' section will also give you details of the original publications.

KEY IDEAS

1

THE
IMAGINARY

Lacan's first important innovation in the field of psychoanalysis took place in 1936, when he was 35 years of age, practising as a psychiatrist and still in psychoanalytic training. At the fourteenth congress of the International Psycho-Analytical Association, held at Marienbad, Lacan presented a paper entitled 'Le stade du miroir', later translated into English as 'The Mirror Stage'. 'The Mirror Stage' remains one of the most frequently anthologized and referenced of Lacan's texts. It was translated as early as 1968 in the Marxist journal *New Left Review* and, as we will see, played a crucial role in the dissemination of Lacanian ideas in film and cultural studies. There is also something of a mythology that has grown around this paper that has been influential in constructing an image of Lacan as an outcast – a heroic figure battling for the truth against a conservative and reactionary establishment.

Ten minutes after starting his presentation on the mirror stage Lacan was interrupted and prevented from continuing by the congress president, Ernest Jones, Freud's biographer and one of his most devoted disciples. Lacan left the congress the following morning and travelled to Berlin where he visited Goebbels' monumental fascist spectacle of the eleventh Olympiad at the newly built Olympic Stadium. In the proceedings of the congress there was only the briefest mention of Lacan's presentation and his paper was not included in the subsequent conference publication. This initial encounter, therefore, can be seen

to set the tone for Lacan's relationship with the psychoanalytic establishment for the rest of his career. He felt himself to have been snubbed
and rejected by the very people he wanted to impress and he responded
in turn by rejecting them. There is certainly some truth in this, and
the International Psycho-Analytical Association remains to this day a
deeply conservative or even, in the eyes of some, reactionary institution. But at the same time we should note that at the congress every
speaker was scheduled to give a ten-minute presentation and by stop-
ping Lacan at the end of his time limit Jones was simply performing his
function as chairperson. Furthermore, Lacan did not submit the paper
for publication in the conference proceedings, so its absence from the
eventual volume cannot be seen as a deliberate exclusion by the IPA.
There is no known transcript of the 1936 paper and the version
included in *Écrits* dates from 1949, when Lacan once more presented
it to the sixteenth international congress of the IPA in Zürich. This time
Lacan was not stopped from speaking and his presentation was
published with the conference proceedings in the *International Journal
of Psycho-Analysis*. Thirteen years had elapsed, therefore, between the
first formulation of Lacan's idea and the paper that we now read – 13
years in which Lacan had continued to develop and modify his ideas.
As Dany Nobus puts it:

> the mirror stage has always been viewed by Lacan as a solid piece of theo-
> rizing, a paradigm retaining its value to explain human self-consciousness,
> aggressivity, rivalry, narcissism, jealousy and fascination with images in
> general. In a sense, this does not come as a surprise when it is appreciated
> that the 1949 *Mirror Stage* article was not something Lacan had concocted at a
> moment's notice, but a pearl which he had carefully cultured for some thirteen
> odd years.

(1998: 104)

CONTEXT AND INFLUENCES

As with all of Lacan's papers, there is a multiplicity of allusions and
references in 'The Mirror Stage', which can often confuse a reader who
is unfamiliar with its context. The paper is concerned with the formation of the ego through the identification with an image of the self.
According to Freud's second model of the mind – what is usually

referred to as the 'topographical' model (see Thurschwell 2000: ch. 5) – the ego represents the organized part of the psyche in contrast to the unorganized elements of the unconscious (the id). As Freud writes, the 'ego is that part of the id which has been modified by the direct influence of the external world. . . . The ego represents what may be called reason and common sense, in contrast to the id, which contains the passions' (Freud 1984a [1923]: 363–4). In this sense, the ego is often associated with consciousness, but this is a mistake. The ego is related to consciousness, but it is also in constant tension with the demands of the unconscious and the imperatives of the superego. The function of the ego, therefore, is defensive insofar as it mediates between the unconscious (the id) and the demands of external reality (the superego). Even at this early stage of his career Lacan was concerned to distinguish the ego from the subject and to elaborate a conception of subjectivity as divided or 'alienated'. Before explaining the detail of his argument, it is important to understand that Lacan drew on a wide range of influences from philosophy and experimental psychology in order to formulate his ideas in this paper. So, I will first briefly highlight four strands of thinking in 'The Mirror Stage': the philosophical tradition of phenomenology; the work of the psychologist Henri Wallon (1879–1962) on mirroring; the work of the ethologist Roger Caillois (1913–78) on mimicry; and the work of philosopher Alexandre Kojève (1902–68) on recognition and desire.

PHENOMENOLOGY

In what we can see as the first phase of Lacan's career – from the completion of his doctoral thesis in 1932 to 'The Rome Discourse' in 1953 (see Chapter 2) – he was philosophically speaking a phenomenologist. Phenomenology derives from the work of the German philosopher Edmund Husserl (1859–1938) and is concerned with the nature of 'pure phenomena', that is to say, with the idea that objects do not exist independently as things in the world separate from our perception of them but are intimately linked to human consciousness. According to phenomenologists, human consciousness is not the passive recognition of material phenomena that are simply there, 'given', but a process of actively constituting or 'intending' those phenomena. Husserl argued that we cannot be certain of anything beyond our immediate experience and therefore have to ignore, or 'put in brackets', everything outside our perception or consciousness. He called this process 'phenomenological reduction' in the sense that we reduce the external world to consciousness alone. In short, the process of thinking about an object and the object itself are mutually dependent. As Terry Eagleton (1983) notes, this is all very abstract and unreal, but the idea behind phenomenology was, paradoxically, to get away from abstract philosophical speculation and get back to the analysis of things themselves in real concrete situations.

Husserl's ideas were further developed by his most famous pupil Martin Heidegger (1889–1976). Heidegger argued that all under-standing is historically situated. As human beings we always perceive the world from a specific situation and our most fundamental desire is to transcend or surpass that situation. This is what Heidegger called the 'project': as a subject one is physically situated in time and space but one then 'projects' oneself into the future. Human sub-jectivity or what we call existence involves this constant process of projecting oneself out on to the world and into the future. For Heidegger, therefore, human consciousness is not an inner world of thoughts and images but a constant process of projecting outside, or what he called 'ex-sistence'. These ideas were carried over to France by Jean-Paul Sartre (1905–80), after he attended Heidegger's lectures in 1932. In an early work entitled *Transcendence of the Ego* (1934) Sartre distinguished between self-consciousness and the ego. As we saw above, Freud defined the ego as the reasoning faculty of the mind, mediating between unconscious passions and external reality. By extending Heidegger's notion of the project Sartre suggested that self-consciousness was essentially 'nothing', while the ego was an object in the world perceived by the subject. In the 1930s and 1940s Lacan was strongly influenced by these ideas. Sartre's distinction between subject and ego paved the way for Lacan's own formulation of the relationship between subject and ego in the mirror stage, while the notions of 'ex-sistence' and 'nothingness' recur throughout his work. What is crucial for understanding Lacan, however, and espe-cially where he adopts ideas from philosophy, anthropology and linguistics, is that he always transforms concepts into a psychoanalytic register. Thus, he transferred phenomenological notions of ex-sistence and nothingness from the realm of consciousness to the unconscious. As Jacques-Alain Miller writes:

> It was essential to him that the unconscious not be taken as an interiority or container in which some drives are found over on the one side and a few identifications over on the other. . . . He took the unconscious not as a container, but rather as something ex-sistent – outside itself – that is connected to a subject who is a lack of being.

(1996: 11)

We will see what Miller means by 'lack of being' below.

EXPERIMENTAL PSYCHOLOGY: THE SELF AS MIRROR IMAGE

Between the first presentation of 'The Mirror Stage' at Marienbad and its publication in 1949, Lacan was preoccupied with the nature of consciousness and specifically self-consciousness. What was it, in other words, that enabled an individual to become aware of him/herself as an autonomous thinking, feeling being in the first place and to maintain this level of self-consciousness? Traditionally psychology had argued that self-awareness arises from the infant's gradual and increasing awareness of its own physical body. The psychologist Henri Wallon argued that this was a rather circular argument in the sense that it presupposed that the infant had a level of individual awareness in the first place in order for it then to become aware of its own body. Consequently, he suggested that the infant must not only gain awareness of its own body and bodily functions but to simultaneously develop an awareness of its environment and the external world in order to differentiate itself from that external environment. In other words, for a person to identify themselves as an autonomous coherent self they must first distinguish themselves from others and from their social environment. A key process in this emergent sense of self, argued Wallon, was the ability of the infant to recognize and simultaneously distinguish itself from its own mirror reflection. The reflected image presents a dilemma for the infant because it is at once intimately connected to its own sense of self and at the same time external to it. Wallon suggested that between the ages of three months and one year the infant gradually progresses from an initial indifference to the mirror image to an acceptance and mastery over this image as separate from itself. What Lacan took from experimental psychology therefore was the importance of the role of mirroring in the construction of self and

of self-consciousness. What psychology could not account for, however, was why the image held this particular fascination and power for
the subject, and for this Lacan turned to a rather different discipline,
ethology, the study of animal behaviour.

It is well known that many small animals and insects can change
their colour to match that of their immediate environment or have
developed particular markings and characteristics to make them indis-
tinguishable from their environment. The usual understanding of this
is that it offers protection for the animals concerned, hiding them from
potential predators. What research tended to show, however, was that
insects that assume the appearance of their environment were just as
likely to be eaten as those that did not. So how could this phenomenon
be explained? In his paper 'Mimicry and Legendary Psychasthenia'
Roger Caillois suggested that, contrary to the usual explanation, insects
that assume the appearance of their environment are in fact assimilating
themselves to that environment. In other words they are captivated
by the very space that surrounds them and seek to lose themselves
within that space, to break down the distinction between organism and
environment. From Caillois' work then Lacan took the idea of the
fascination and capturing properties of the image and above all how
we shape ourselves according to that image. Lacan's innovation in
'The Mirror Stage' was to combine the phenomenological distinction
between subject and ego with a psychological understanding of the
role of images and the constructed nature of the self through the philosophical category of the dialectic.

THE DIALECTIC OF RECOGNITION AND DESIRE

Between 1933 and 1939 the philosopher Alexandre Kojève conducted
a weekly seminar on the philosophy of G.W.F. Hegel (1770–1831).
Kojève's influential seminar was attended by almost all the major
figures of France's immediate post-war intellectual life – Jean-Paul
Sartre, Maurice Merleau-Ponty and Georges Bataille to name just a
few – including Lacan himself. Kojève's interpretation of Hegel was
to have a profound influence on this whole generation of thinkers and
dominated French philosophy until the mid-1960s, when Hegelianism
was finally displaced by Structuralism and Post-structuralism. Hegel

elaborated a complex philosophical system based on a form of thinking known as *dialectics*.

Dialectics are a mode of philosophical thought that stresses the interconnectedness of phenomena and the unity of opposites. This is often represented schematically as 'thesis – anti-thesis – synthesis', where each idea generates its opposite and the unity of two produces a new level of understanding or analysis. For example, the idea of the individual subject – the 'self' (thesis) – only makes sense in relation to another subject – an 'other' (anti-thesis). Once we begin to understand that the self is intricately connected to the other and cannot exist without the other we have a new concept, a collective 'we' subject (synthesis). This moment of synthesis then becomes a new thesis generating its own anti-thesis and so on. Dialectical thought, therefore, foregrounds the contradictory nature of all things, as all phenomena can be said to contain their opposite; their own negation. Out of this relationship or unity of opposites something new will emerge in an endless process of transformation.

Kojève was particularly interested in Hegel's account of the emergence of self-consciousness as an account of the transition from nature to culture, or to put it another way, as the transition from animal existence to human existence. According to Hegel, self-hood emerges through a process of developing self-consciousness through the activity of self-reflection. For the human subject to emerge it must not simply be conscious of its own distinctiveness but must be recognized as a human subject by another. Hegel sketched out this process as the dialectic of 'Lordship and Bondage', more commonly known as the 'Master/Slave' dialectic. In this account two subjects – a 'Master' and a 'Slave' – are apparently locked in a reciprocal relationship of recognition. In order for the Master to be a subject he must be recognized by the Slave as such; in turn, the Slave knows he is a Slave because he is recognized by the Master as one. The Master is thus free to pursue his life in the firm knowledge that his identity is affirmed by the recognition of the Slave. The paradox of the dialectic, however, is that a positive always turns into a negative. Because the Master is dependent upon the Slave for the recognition of his identity he can never be truly 'free', whereas the Slave is not dependent on the Master in the same way because he has another source of self-affirmation, his work. If the Slave's identity is affirmed through his work as a Slave, it is not the Master who is free but the Slave.

Kojève read this dialectic as essentially a struggle of desire and recognition. The Master and the Slave are locked in a mutual struggle for recognition: neither can exist without the recognition of the other, but at the same time the other also requires his/her own recognition. It is then for Kojève a struggle to the death, but the death of one will also be the death of the other. The Master and the Slave are locked within a struggle whereby one cannot do without the other but at the same time each is the other's worst enemy. It is this dialectic, according to Lacan, that permeates the imaginary. Moreover, this dialectic introduces into the psychological account of mirroring outlined above the element of *aggressivity*, that is to say, it posits the relationship between self and other as fundamentally conflictual. It was Hegel's great insight, contends Lacan, to reveal how 'each human being is in the being of the other' (Lacan 1988b [1978]: 72). We are caught in a reciprocal and irreducible dialectic of *alienation*. There are, however, two moments of alienation for Lacan, first, through the mirror phase and the formation of the ego, and, second, through language and the constitution of the subject. We will look at the first moment of alienation below and return to the second in the following chapter.

THE MIRROR STAGE

The mirror phase occurs roughly between the ages of six and 18 months and corresponds to Freud's stage of primary narcissism. That is the stage of human development when the subject is in love with the image of themselves and their own bodies and which precedes the love of others (see Thurschwell 2000: ch. 5). Between the ages of six and 18 months the infant begins to recognize his/her image in the mirror (this does not mean a literal mirror but rather any reflective surface, for example the mother's face) and this is usually accompanied by pleasure. The child is fascinated with its image and tries to control and play with it. Although the child initially confuses its image with reality, he/she soon recognizes that the image has its own properties, finally accepting that the image is their own image – a reflection of themselves.

During the mirror stage, then, the child for the first time becomes aware, through seeing its image in the mirror, that his/her body has a total form. The infant can also govern the movements of this image through the movements of its own body and thus experiences pleasure. This sense of completeness and mastery, however, is in contrast to the child's experience of its own body, over which it does not yet have full motor control. While the infant still feels his/her body to be in parts, as fragmented and not yet unified, it is the image that provides him/her with a sense of unification and wholeness. The mirror image, therefore, anticipates the mastery of the infant's own body and stands in contrast to the feelings of fragmentation the infant experiences. What is important at this point is that the infant *identifies* with this mirror image. The image is him/herself. This identification is crucial, as without it – and without the anticipation of mastery that it establishes – the infant would never get to the stage of perceiving him/herself as a complete or whole being. At the same time, however, the image is *alienating* in the sense that it becomes confused with the self. The image actually comes to take the place of the self. Therefore, the sense of a unified self is acquired at the price of this self being an-other, that is, our mirror image. Lacan describes it like this:

> The *mirror stage* is a drama whose internal thrust is precipitated from insufficiency to anticipation – and which manufactures for all the subject, caught up in the lure of spatial identification, the succession of phantasies that extends from a fragmented body-image to a form of its totality that I shall call orthopaedic – and, lastly, to the assumption of the armour of an alienating identity, which will mark with its rigid structure the infants entire mental development.
>
> (1977a [1949]: 4)

For Lacan, the ego emerges at this moment of alienation and fascination with one's own image. The ego is both formed by and takes its form from the organizing and constituting properties of the image. The ego is the effect of images; it is, in short, an imaginary function. Lacan is arguing here against Ego psychology and its tendency to prioritize the ego over unconscious processes as well as to equate the ego with the self. Lacan insists that the ego is based on an illusory image of wholeness and mastery and it is the function of the ego to maintain this illusion of coherence and mastery. The function of the ego is, in other words, one of *mis-recognition*; of refusing to accept the truth of fragmentation and alienation.

According to Lacan, from the moment the image of unity is posited in opposition to the experience of fragmentation, the subject is established as a rival to itself. A conflict is produced between the infant's fragmented sense of self and the imaginary autonomy out of which the ego is born. The same rivalry established between the subject and him/herself is also established in future relations between the subject and others. As Benvenuto and Kennedy put it, 'the primary conflict between identification with, and primordial rivalry with, the other's image, begins a dialectical process that links the ego to more complex social situations' (1986: 58). To exist one has to be recognized by an-other. But this means that our image, which is equal to ourselves, is mediated by the gaze of the other. The other, then, becomes the guarantor of ourselves. We are at once dependent on the other as the guarantor of our own existence and a bitter rival to that same other.

Critics of Lacan's mirror stage argue that he in fact has things completely the wrong way round. In order for the subject to identify with an image in the mirror and then to mis-recognize themselves, they must first have a sense of themselves as a self. If the Lacanian subject is an alienated subject then this presupposes a 'non-alienated' subject in the first instance, otherwise there is nothing that one can meaningfully be said to be alienated from. Hence, the idea of a primary lack or absence is based upon the presupposition of a primary presence or unity. Lack in this sense is secondary and not primary. Anthony Elliott argues that the very terms of Lacan's mirror stage are all wrong: mirror reflection, lack and absence are not pre-existing phenomena but the work of the subject and the imaginary (see Elliott 1998: ch. 4). Lacan's use of the term alienation is rather different from that of his critics though. Through the mirror stage the infant imagines that it achieves mastery over its own body but in a place outside of itself. Alienation, in Lacan, is precisely this 'lack of being' through which the infant's realization (in both senses of the term: forming a distinct concept in the mind and becoming real) lies in an-other place. In this sense, the subject is not alienated *from* something or from itself but rather alienation is constitutive of the subject – the subject is alienated *in* its very being.

THE MIRROR, THE SCREEN AND THE SPECTATOR

As we saw above 'The Mirror Stage' was one of the first articles by Lacan to be translated into English and it was extremely influential in literary and cultural studies, paving the way for a more widespread acceptance of Lacanian ideas. From a literary perspective Lacan's conception of the imaginary and the formation of the ego has been utilized to give an account of both the construction of identity and subjectivity within texts as well as the relationships between characters (see Parkin-Gounelas 2001: ch. 1). It has been in film studies, though, that the notion of the imaginary has had the greatest impact. Lacan's mirror stage was seen to correspond to the relationship between film spectators and the image projected on to the screen. Probably the most important early essay to incorporate Lacanian psychoanalysis into film theory was Jean-Louis Baudry's 'Ideological Effects of the Basic Cinematographic Apparatus', first published in *Cinethique* in 1970. Baudry's article was concerned with the way in which cinematographic apparatus – that is to say, the instruments and technical base of film production, projection and consumption – is constitutive of meaning in its own right. According to Baudry, the significance or meaning of a specific film does not lie in the content of the story presented but rather in the whole set-up of cinematic spectatorship. This shift in the use of psychoanalysis from interpreting the content of individual texts to an analysis of how our subjectivity and identity are constructed through the structure and form of texts has been arguably the most important contribution of Lacanianism to contemporary cultural studies. Let us now see how Baudry used Lacan's concepts before turning to the critique of them.

According to Baudry, the cinematic apparatus constructs our position as film spectators through the position of the camera and the process of projection. The camera occupies both the position from which the images we see on the screen are shot and the position from which we subsequently see those images. The camera therefore situates both the objects of perception (the images on the screen) and the perceiving subject (the film spectator). In this double sense the apparatus of cinema locates us as film spectators and directs our gaze in a very specific way. What makes film different, however, from other forms of images that we see on a daily basis, such as advertisements, paintings or photographic images, is that film presents us not with an isolated image but with a succession of images. The function of the projector and the screen is to restore to that sequence of images the sense of continuity of movement necessary for us to construct meaning out of it. According to Baudry, it is the subject, the film spectator, who makes the necessary links and connections between the series of images displayed before him/her in order for these discrete images to become meaningful as a whole sequence. Therefore, continuity is an attribute of the subject and the subject's relationship to the images on the screen rather than of the film plot.

In this sense, the cinematic subject is formed through the function of the camera, the projector and the screen. It is in relation to the complex process of identification that exists between the spectator and image on the screen that apparatus theory draws most heavily on psychoanalytic ideas. Baudry describes film spectators in Lacanian terms as being placed in a darkened and enclosed space in which, whether they know it or not (and they usually do not), they are 'chained, captured or captivated' (1974–5: 45). What interests Baudry is the way in which Lacan's mirror or reflective surface is framed, limited and circumscribed. You will recall that the primary site of identification in the imaginary is the body itself, that this process takes place in front of a reflective surface before which the infant has only limited mobility, and that there is also an element of confusion for the infant between the reality of their own experience and the image before them. As with the imaginary, the cinematic mirror-screen reflects back images but not reality, although a reflection must always be a reflection of something. Identification, Baudry argues, takes place on two distinct levels in the cinematic process. First, the spectator identifies with what is represented on the screen – the events, characters etc. Second, the spectator identifies with the camera itself and it is the latter of these that is most important. For Baudry, the content of specific films is not really significant; it is the process that matters. Film and the cinematic apparatus, therefore, enacts the Lacanian dialectic of absence and presence. The preconditions for cinematic identification to take place are also the two preconditions for the imaginary and the mirror stage to take place, that is to say, the suspension of mobility and the primacy of the visual function. Baudry thus concluded his essay with the suggestion that the cinematic spectator is formed precisely in the same way as Lacan's divided and alienated subject. As we will now see there are a number of problems with Baudry's work. These problems were drawn out by one of the most important psychoanalytic film theorists of the 1970s and 1980s, Christian Metz, as well as by feminist film theorists, such as Laura Mulvey.

CHRISTIAN METZ'S CRITIQUE OF BAUDRY

Christian Metz accepts Baudry's thesis that the primary identification of the spectator revolves around the camera rather than the images represented on the screen, but he questions whether or not this can be equated with Lacan's mirror stage. There is a sense, he suggests, in which we can see the process of cinematic identification as analogous to the mirror stage, but this is not a very precise sense. Metz points out that what the child sees in the mirror and identifies with is an image of its own body, and that it identifies itself as an object. In the traditional cinema, on the other hand, what the spectator sees on the screen is not an image of her or himself. Indeed, for Metz, the precondition for the spectator to recognise their absence from the screen or

the intelligible unfolding of the film despite that absence – is the fact the spectator has already known the experience of the mirror (the true mirror), and is thus able to constitute a world of objects without having first to recognise himself within it.

(1982: 46)

In this sense the cinema should be located not in Lacan's imaginary order but in the symbolic order (see Chapter 2).

Metz defines identification with either characters or actors as secondary identification. The primary identification of the cinema is not with something that is *seen* (as in the mirror stage) but with something *seeing*, as Metz puts it, 'a pure, all-seeing and invisible subject' (1982: 97). What is seen in this situation – the object on the screen – does not know it is being seen and it is this lack of awareness in the object that it is seen that facilitates the voyeuristic quality of the cinema. Film spectators are essentially voyeurs without being aware that they are voyeurs. Metz insists on the need to maintain a separation cinema and psychoanalysis. What psychoanalysis provides film studies with are the concepts through which we can understand how cinema works, especially notions of scopophilia (the overwhelming desire to look) and fetishism. We will see how these concepts work in our discussion of feminist film criticism in 'After Lacan'. First, we must consider one more groundbreaking article.

LAURA MULVEY AND VISUAL PLEASURE

For both Baudry and Metz the cinematic spectator was conceived of as essentially a male voyeur. In an incredibly influential essay, 'Visual Pleasure and Narrative Cinema', Laura Mulvey took up these debates and argued that the cinema produces a fundamentally male gaze or look and that the woman is always the object of this gaze. Mulvey suggested that there were three levels upon which the gaze operated in the cinema. First, there is the gaze of the camera as it is filming and this, following Metz, is always a voyeuristic gaze. Second, there are the looks intrinsic to the film narrative and these are usually the looks of male protagonists, as they position women characters within the narrative itself. Finally, there is the gaze of the spectator, and, as this gaze is facilitated by the previous two positions – of the camera and of the protagonists within the film – it is an inherently male position to adopt. Mulvey's formulation of the 'male gaze' provided the starting point for many debates around the possibility of elaborating feminine, black and gay spectator positions. Would women always remain the object of the spectacle or does Lacanian psychoanalysis offer alternative ways out? We will see how Lacanians addressed this issue in subsequent chapters.

SUMMARY

In 'The Mirror Stage' Lacan draws on an extraordinary range of sources from philosophy, psychology and ethology, to reformulate the psychoanalytic conception of the ego and the imaginary. The imaginary is the realm of the ego, a pre-linguistic realm of sense perception, identification and an illusory sense of unity. The primary relation in the imaginary is a relation with one's own body, that is to say, the specular image of the body itself. These imaginary processes form the ego and are repeated and reinforced by the subject in his/her relationship with the external world. The imaginary, therefore, is not a developmental phase – it is not something that one goes through and grows out of – but remains at the core of our experience. As the sense of original unity and coherence in the mirror phase is an illusion, there is a fundamental disharmony regarding the ego. The ego is essentially a terrain of conflict and discord; a site of continual struggle. What Lacan refers to as a 'lack of being' is this ontological gap or primary loss at the very heart of our subjectivity. Lacan goes further, however, than just suggesting that we have lost an original sense of unity; he argues that this loss is constitutive of subjectivity itself. In short, the imaginary is a realm of identification and mirror-reflection; a realm of distortion and illusion. It is a realm in which a futile struggle takes place on the part of the ego to once more attain an imaginary unity and coherence.

2

THE SYMBOLIC

If 'The Mirror Stage' represented Lacan's first innovation within the field of psychoanalysis, it was one that remained recognizably within the limits of accepted theory and practice. It was almost 15 years before a distinctively Lacanian reading of psychoanalysis began to emerge when, in 1951, Lacan made his call for a 'return to Freud'. Two years later, at the Rome Congress of Romance Language Psychoanalysts, Lacan delivered a paper entitled 'The Function and Field of Speech and Language in Psychoanalysis' (1977b [1956]), subsequently known as 'The Rome Discourse'. This paper set out his major concerns for the following decade, the distinction between speech and language, an understanding of the *subject* as distinct from the *I* and, above all, the elaboration of the central concepts of the *signifier* and the *symbolic order*. Also in 1953, Lacan and a group of colleagues left the Paris Psycho-Analytical Society to form the Société Française de Psychanalyse (SFP). The Rome Discourse came to be seen as the founding document of the new school and of a new direction in psychoanalysis.

This chapter focuses upon Lacan's work in the 1950s, when he placed his greatest emphasis on the role of language in psychoanalysis and formulated his most important thesis: that *the unconscious is structured like a language*. This was an extraordinarily innovative period for Lacan and he introduced many of the concepts that would preoccupy him for the rest of his career. In order to help you understand these concepts and Lacan's transformation of them, this chapter will outline the major influences from this period and show how Lacan drew on a field of study known as *Structuralism* and on linguistic theory. In so doing the chapter provides the framework for a more detailed discussion of the unconscious and the subject in the following chapter. I will briefly introduce Structuralism before outlining Claude Lévi-Strauss's (1908–) elementary structure of kinship, as this provides the basis for understanding Lacan's conception of the symbolic order and the formation of the unconscious. Lévi-Strauss's structural anthropology was facilitated by the work of the Swiss linguist Ferdinand de Saussure (1857–1913) and it was through Lévi-Strauss that Lacan began to read linguistics. In the process he made radical and far-reaching changes to Saussure's concept of the linguistic sign, completely reversing any conventional understanding of the relationship between the speaking subject and language. Finally, we will look at the Russian linguist Roman Jakobson's (1896–1982) work on metaphor and metonymy, as this was crucially important for Lacan's conceptualization of *desire*. Exploring these influences will help you understand Lacan's conception of the subject as constituted in and through language. The chapter concludes with Lacan's analysis of Edgar Allan Poe's short story *The Purloined Letter* as this clearly illustrates what he calls the subject as *the subject of the signifier*.

STRUCTURALISM

Structuralism was first and foremost a method of analysis that dominated French intellectual life in the 1950s and 1960s. It was not a movement as such but rather a label for a mode of thinking and analysis common to a wide range of disciplines, from mathematics to literary criticism. Structuralism was seen to be applicable to all human social phenomena. The disparate collection of thinkers who are now placed, frequently incorrectly, under the rubric *Structuralism* do not form a coherent group. These often include the psychologist Jean Piaget (1896–1980); the linguist Roman Jakobson (1896–1982); the literary theorists Roland Barthes (1915–80), Tzvetan Todorov (1939–) and Gérard Genette (1930–); the social theorist Michel Foucault (1926–84); the Marxist philosopher Louis Althusser (1918–90); and, of course, the psychoanalyst Jacques Lacan. The sources of Structuralism were very eclectic and its influence wide ranging, but it has now inextricably come to be associated with the work of a single figure, the anthropologist Claude Lévi-Strauss.

Lévi-Strauss's structural methodology derives from Saussure's foundational distinction between *langue* and *parole* (see p. 37) or the distinction between a given system, such as language, and the individual expression or manifestation of that system, as in an individual's speech. Structuralists were not concerned with the meaning of individual signs but with describing the organization of the overall sign-system or 'structure'. Linguistics provided the model for this form of analysis, although the main objects of study for Structuralism were very often non-verbal sign systems; for example, Roland Barthes' study of fashion (1985 [1967]), or Lévi-Strauss's own analysis of kinship systems (1969 [1949]) and food preparation (1966). The basic premise of Structuralism was that all social activity constitutes a language insofar as it involves sign systems with their own intrinsic rules and grammar. Thus, we understand individual acts not in their own right but against a background of social relations from which they derive their meaning.

THE SYMBOLIC FUNCTION

In his seminal study 'The Elementary Structures of Kinship' (1969 [1949]) Lévi-Strauss analysed the marriage and kinship systems of so-called 'primitive' societies. He postulated that what one found in the marriage relations of these societies was nothing less than the basic underlying structure of society itself; in other words, the elementary structure from which all subsequent social relations derive. What is important about Lévi-Strauss's study is not so much its accuracy, as his notion of elementary structures has been widely disputed and disproved, but rather the nature of the study itself. Lévi-Strauss argued that what was significant in this process was not so much the exchange of real people – of actual women – but the way in which women were transformed into signs and operated within a system of *symbolic exchange*. The exchange of women operated like a language – a formal system with its own rules and regulations which could not be infringed but at the same time remained unconscious to the individual system users. In other words, there is an unconscious structure that determines people's social position and regulates their relationships without their being aware of it. Lacan drew two important lessons from Lévi-Strauss:

1   That there is an elementary structure – a single 'unconscious' structure – which can be seen to underlie all other kinship and social relations.

2   That what takes place within kinship systems is not the giving and taking of real persons in marriage but a process of symbolic exchange.

From the structural anthropology of Lévi-Strauss, therefore, Lacan derives the idea that what characterises the human world is the *symbolic function* – a function that intervenes in all aspects of our lives. Furthermore, in an introduction to the work of another anthropologist, Marcel Mauss (1872–1950), Lévi-Strauss suggested that 'what is called the unconscious is merely an empty space in which the symbolic function achieves autonomy', that is to say, a space where 'symbols are more real than what they symbolize' (Roudinesco 1999: 211). In the 1950s Lacan wanted to re-establish psychoanalysis as a science and, in order to do so, he first had to identify what was specific about its object of study, the unconscious, and how one could go about studying it. Lévi-Strauss's insight into the autonomy of the symbolic function was to provide Lacan with a crucial step in his attempt to establish Freudian psychoanalysis on a more philosophically and scientifically firm footing. But to make this move fully Lacan needed to make one more theoretical detour – a detour through linguistics.

SAUSSURE (1857–1913) AND THE LINGUISTIC SIGN

Ferdinand de Saussure's *Cours de linguistique générale* (published posthumously in 1916, see 1983) has been described as nothing less than a 'Copernican revolution' in the human and social sciences, in the sense that, 'instead of men's words being seen as peripheral to men's understanding of reality, men's understanding of reality came to be seen as revolving about their social use of verbal signs' (Saussure 1983 [1916]: ix). Prior to Saussure the study of language was primarily concerned with philology and etymology, that is to say, tracing the history and derivation of words. Traditionally linguistics saw language as composed of separate discrete units or words, each word having its own 'meaning' adhering to it. Saussure argued that if linguistics was to be considered scientific it could not be based upon historical principles, or what is termed a *diachronic* approach. Scientific method requires that one first identifies one's object of study. In terms of linguistics this required the linguist to view language not historically but *synchronically* as a system that is complete at any given moment in time. In this system all the elements and rules are, in theory at least, simultaneously available to the language user. When we use language we do so against a background of vocabulary, syntax, grammar and conventions; we are not conscious of all those elements when we speak or write but they are there and they determine what we can and cannot say. If we transgress the rules, our speech becomes meaningless.

Saussure distinguished three aspects of language:

- Language itself as a universal human phenomenon of communication.
- *Langue* as a particular language or language system (English, for example).
- *Parole* as language in use, specific speech acts or utterances.

His work was concerned with the second of these categories, that is, language as a system and how meaning is created by that system. What is important here, and particularly in relation to Lacan, is that individual speaking subjects remain unconscious of the system itself. Saussure's most original contribution to the study of language, then, was the conception of language as a *total system* – a system that governs what people can say, while they themselves remain unconscious of its rules.

According to Saussure, language is not simply a list of terms that correspond to a set of things, or phenomena, in the world. Language is rather a system of *signs*. A 'correspondence' theory of language sees it as a system of signs that refers directly to objects in the world. We can diagrammatically represent this through the relationship between a *word* – its *concept* or idea – and the thing to which it refers, the *referent*:

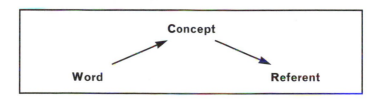

Saussure argued, however, that words cannot refer to specific phenomena in the material world, as this assumes that there is a natural, organic, relation between words and what they represent. As he pointed out, if I speak the word 'tree' or 'chair' we will all immediately conjure up conceptions of trees or chairs, but these images do not actually refer to a specific tree or chair in the material world. Instead, we are all thinking about different trees and chairs. What the word 'tree' refers to is not a 'thing' – a real tree – but a concept of a tree. We must, therefore, bracket the term 'referent' and put the notion that language refers to substantive phenomena in the real world to one side. Our diagram now looks like this:

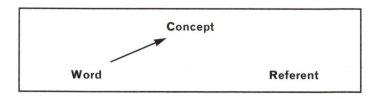

The word does not refer to a specific referent at all, but only to a concept, and the proper concern of linguistics – the linguistic sign – consists of a word and its concept. Saussure's linguistic sign consists of two elements: the sound pattern or written word, which is called the *signifier*, and the concept, which is known as the *signified*. Again this can be sketched diagrammatically as:

Sign →
Signified [Concept]

Signifier [Sound pattern/word image]

The relationship between the signifier and the signified is arbitrary and is determined by social convention. But if language does not correspond to objects in the world then how does it become meaningful? According to Saussure, meaning does not reside in individual signs but in the relationship between signs in the language system itself. Language creates a differential system whereby any given sign acquires its meaning by virtue of its difference from other signs. When we speak we choose to use certain words and exclude others. For example, I may say 'chair' rather than 'throne' or 'armchair'. Each word designates a piece of furniture I can sit upon but they all have very different meanings. This element of selection is called the *paradigmatic* axis of language. But I cannot select and use any word I want. I must combine them in a syntactically correct way for them to make sense and this is referred to as the *syntagmatic* axis. The meaning of each word, each sign, also depends on the words that come before and after it in a sentence. Let us take, for example, the sentence:

We will leave Paris tomorrow.

Each term in this sentence acquires its meaning on the one hand through its differentiation from other possible terms we could use in the same context and on the other through its place in the overall sentence structure. Thus, 'We' could be substituted by 'I', 'you', 'he' or 'she', or 'tomorrow' could be substituted by 'today'. The sentence will still make sense if we substitute these terms but it will have a very different meaning. These alternatives are absent from the immediate situation of language use but are present as a background against which we understand specific terms. Second, the meaning of a sentence arises from a specific combination of terms rather than its individual elements in isolation. Thus, if we rearranged this sentence we can still understand the individual terms but it does not make sense overall:

Paris leave will tomorrow we.

This is the function of syntax and grammar or the syntagmatic axis. Language works by combining these two functions; the meaning of what a person says depends not only upon the words they use and those they exclude but also upon the place of those words within an overall structure.

Language exists as a complex network of signs. A given sign is defined not by virtue of an intrinsic value or meaning, but rather through its relative position within the overall system of signification and through its difference from all the other signs in that system. A sign does not refer us to a specific object in the real material world, but rather to another sign which in turn refers us to another sign and so on.

$$\frac{\text{Signified}}{\text{Signifier}} \rightarrow \frac{\text{Signified}}{\text{Signifier}} \rightarrow \frac{\text{Signified}}{\text{Signifier}} \rightarrow \frac{\text{Signified}}{\text{Signifier}}$$

A good example of this is the use of a dictionary. If we want to find out what a word means, what do we do? We look it up in a dictionary. But a dictionary is simply a compendium of signs; therefore, the meaning of a specific sign is simply another sign and if we were to look up the meaning of this second sign we would find another and another and so on and so forth. This process will never come to a stop at an actual referent in the real world, but results in an endless process of 'signification'.

There are three essential lessons to be drawn from Saussure's theory of language:

* Language precedes consciousness; as speaking subjects we are born into language.
* Language does not reflect reality but rather one produces one's experience within the constraints of the given language system and that language system, to some extent, conditions the nature of one's experience.
* Language is not an absolute and fixed system within which a singular meaning can be located, but it is rather a set of differential relations.

Saussure's conception of language as a total system provided the model for Lévi-Strauss's concept of structure and in turn Lacan's symbolic order. But there is an important difference between Lacan and Saussure. For Saussure, the two halves of the sign are always inextricably bound together – like two sides of a sheet of paper – and cannot be separated. Taking his cue from Lévi-Strauss's reflection on the autonomy of the symbolic function, it was precisely the indivisibility of the sign that Lacan brought into question.

THE PRIMACY OF THE SIGNIFIER

Lacan accepted the arbitrary nature of the linguistic sign but questioned two of the fundamental premises of Saussurean linguistics: the indivisibility of the sign and the prioritization of the signified over the signifier. In a famous example from 'The Agency of the Letter in the Unconscious, or Reason Since Freud' (1977c [1957]) Lacan dismisses the usual Saussurean illustration of the functioning of the sign, that is, the picture of a tree, and replaces it with another:

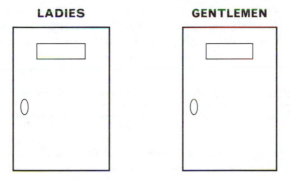

Lacan then proceeds to tell this story:

> A train arrives at a station. A little boy and a little girl, brother and sister, are seated in a compartment face to face next to the window through which the buildings along the station platform can be seen passing as the train pulls to a stop. 'Look', says the brother, 'we're at Ladies!'; 'Idiot!' replies his sister, 'Can't you see we're at Gentlemen'.

(1977c [1957]: 152)

What this example reveals, argues Lacan, is the way in which the signifier enters the signified. The doors are identical, so what distinguishes one toilet door from the other is nothing except the signifier above the doors. What Lacan is proposing, therefore, is to reverse the priority Saussure bestowed upon the signified in the signifier/signified relation. Lacan's reformulation now reads:

Signifier

---

signified

The capitalized Signifier takes precedence over the signified and the 'bar' between the two elements symbolizes, for Lacan, not the inseparability of the sign but its fundamental division. The bar functions as a barrier to meaning. What a signifier refers to is not a signified, as there is always a barrier between them, but to another signifier. In short, a signifier refers us to another signifier, which in turn refers us to another signifier in an almost endless chain of signification. If we try to define the meaning of a specific word or concept, for example, we can only do so through other words; we are caught in a continual process of producing signs. Our schematic representation of the language system given above could therefore be rewritten as:

$$\frac{\text{Signifier}}{\text{signified}} \rightarrow \frac{\text{Signifier}}{\text{signified}} \rightarrow \frac{\text{Signifier}}{\text{signified}} \rightarrow \frac{\text{Signifier}}{\text{signified}}$$

Signification is always a process – a chain. None of its elements actually 'consist' of the meaning or the signified but rather each signifier 'insists' on a meaning, as it presses forward to the next signifier. Meaning is not fixed, or as Lacan puts it, there is 'an incessant sliding of the signified under the signifier' (1977c [1957]: 154). Lacan, however, is not suggesting that there is no 'fixed' meaning at all. There are what he called 'anchoring points' or '*points de caption*', where this incessant sliding of the signified under the signifier stops and allows for moments of stable signification. The *point de caption* literally designates an upholstery button of the kind one finds on sofas and mattresses and which are used to hold the stuffing in place. Saussure's 'scientific', as opposed to historical, analysis of language provided Lacan with a model to study Freud's 'talking-cure'. Saussure revealed how there was a 'structure' within us that governed what we say; for Lacan that structure *is* the unconscious. The unconscious is at once produced through language and governed by the rules of language. The precise mechanism through which this takes place was provided by Roman Jakobson.

ROMAN JAKOBSON (1896–1982)

Jakobson took up Saussure's distinction between the two axes of language – the paradigmatic and the syntagmatic – and proposed a correspondence between these axes and the rhetorical figures of metaphor and metonymy. Metaphor is the use of a word or expression to describe something else without stating a direct comparison. Metonymy, on the other hand, is the use of a term for one thing applied to something else with which it is usually associated, for example, when one says 'crown' for the position of the monarch, or 'sail' to imply a boat. Jakobson pointed out that metaphor is an act of *substitution* of one term for another and thus corresponded to the paradigmatic axis, or the axis of selection. Metonymy is a relation of *contiguity*, in that one term refers to another because it is associated or adjacent to it, and therefore it corresponds to the syntagmatic axis, or the axis of combination. Lacan saw in Jakobson's structural model of metaphor and metonymy a direct correspondence with Freud's processes of dream work: *condensation* and *displacement*. Condensation designates the process whereby two or more signs or images in a dream are combined to form a composite image that is then invested with the meaning of both its constitutive elements. In persecutory dreams, for example, the dreamer may dream that they are being punished by an unknown authority figure and try to identify that figure with someone in their life. This figure may well in fact not be a single person, however, but a composite, or condensation, of a number of different persons – parental figures, employer or partner. All of the ambivalent feelings that the dreamer has around these figures combine into a single persecutor in the dream. Displacement describes the process through which meaning is transferred from one sign to another. Let us take the example of anxiety dreams. In anxiety dreams the dreamer may become anxious about some very minor incident in their lives, but this functions as simply a way of avoiding, or displacing, a much more serious problem that they are facing. These two processes are what Freud called *primary processes* in contrast to the *secondary processes* of conscious thought. By mapping Jakobson's distinction between metaphor and metonymy on to Freud's *primary processes* Lacan was finally able to demonstrate how the unconscious was structured like a language. The unconscious, he argued, operates according to the rules of metaphor and metonymy.

THE SYMBOLIC ORDER

Throughout the 1950s Lacan was concerned with elaborating a system according to which everything in the human world is structured 'in accordance with the symbols which have emerged' (Lacan 1988b [1978]: 29). Lacan is not saying here that everything is reducible to the symbolic, but that, once symbols have appeared, everything will be ordered, or structured, in accordance with those symbols and the laws of the symbolic, *including* the unconscious and human subjectivity. For Freud, the unconscious is that part of our existence that escapes us and over which we have no control, but at the same time which governs our thoughts and wishes. For Lacan, on the other hand, the unconscious consists of signifying material. The unconscious is a process of signification that is beyond our control; it is the language that speaks through us rather than the language we speak. In this sense, Lacan defines the unconscious as the discourse of the Other. The big Other is language, the symbolic order; this Other can never be fully assimilated to the subject; it is a radical otherness which, nevertheless, forms the core of our unconscious. We will see how this works in the following chapter, but first let us look at Lacan's conception of the subject and how it is determined by the signifier.

Lacan conceived of the symbolic order as a totalizing concept in the sense that it marks the limit of the human universe. We are born into language – the language through which the desires of others are articulated and through which we are forced to articulate our own desire. We are locked within what Lacan calls a circuit of discourse:

> It is the discourse of the circuit in which I am integrated. I am one of its links. It is the discourse of my father, for instance, in so far as my father made mistakes which I am condemned to reproduce. . . . I am condemned to reproduce them because I am obliged to pick up again the discourse he bequeathed to me, not simply because I am his son, but because one can't stop the chain of discourse, and it is precisely my duty to transmit it in its aberrant form to someone else.
>
> (Lacan 1988b [1978]: 89)

We are born into this circuit of discourse; it marks us before our birth and will continue after our death. To be fully human we are *subjected* to this symbolic order – the order of language, of discourse; we cannot escape it, although as a structure it escapes us. As individual subjects, we can never fully grasp the social or symbolic totality that constitutes the sum of our universe, but that totality has a structuring force upon us as subjects.

In the previous chapter we saw how Lacan distinguished between the ego and the subject. The ego is an 'imaginary function' formed primarily through the subject's relationship to their own body. The subject, on the other hand, is constituted in the symbolic order and is determined by language. There is always a disjunction, according to Lacan, between the subject of enunciation and the subject of the utterance; in other words, the subject who speaks and the subject who is spoken. Following the linguist Emile Benveniste's (1902–76) conception of 'I' as a *shifter* – as having no specific referent but in the act of speech designating the person who says 'I' – Lacan argued that the 'I' in speech does not refer to anything stable in language at all. The 'I' can be occupied by a number of different phenomena: the subject, the ego or the unconscious. For example, in what Lacan called 'empty speech', the 'I' would correspond to the ego; in 'full speech' it corresponds to the subject; while at other times it corresponds to neither subject nor ego. This is what Lacan means when he says *I is an other*, that is to say, 'I' is not 'me'; these two terms do not refer to the same entity; the subject is not the same as the individual person – it is de-centred in relation to the individual. In short, Lacan *de-essentializes* the 'I' and prioritizes the symbolic, the signifier, over the subject. It is the structure of language that speaks the subject and not the other way around. Lacan summarizes this in his famous statement, *the subject is that which is represented by one signifier to another*. The seminar on *The Purloined Letter* is nothing less than an exposition of this, whereby the subject is caught up in the chain of signification and it is the signifier that marks the subject, that defines the subject's position within the symbolic order.

THE PURLOINED LETTER

Lacan's seminar on *The Purloined Letter* was first delivered in 1954. It was written up the following year and formed the introductory essay to the original French publication of the *Écrits*, although it was removed from later editions. As Benvenuto and Kennedy point out, placing the seminar on Poe at the beginning of the *Écrits* served a dual function: it both represented what was to follow and, more importantly, it established a particular mode of reading. In 'order to read Lacan, the story seems to be saying, one must follow the path of the signifier, and the remainder of *Écrits* is fundamentally concerned with the laws of the signifier' (Benvenuto and Kennedy 1986: 23–4). The 1954–5 seminar series was given the overall title *The Ego in Freud's Theory and in the Technique of Psychoanalysis* and concerned Freud's late metapsychological text *Beyond the Pleasure Principle* (1984b [1920]). Lacan was primarily concerned with Freud's idea of repetition compulsion, that is, the compulsive urge to repeat unpleasant experiences in apparent disregard of the pleasure principle. Lacan called this process 'repetition automatism' and associated it with his idea of the insistence of the signifying chain. Lacan's seminar on *The Purloined Letter* is an illustration of this thesis, that is, *the insistence of the signifying chain and the determination of the subject by the signifier*.

Edgar Allan Poe's (1809–49) short story *The Purloined Letter* was the final tale in a trilogy about the detective, M. Dupin. The story concerns the theft of a letter from the Queen by one of the King's Ministers and the search for this letter first, unsuccessfully, by the police and then, successfully, by Dupin. The twist in Poe's story is that the letter is in fact never hidden but always in full disclosure. According to Lacan, the tale can be divided into two scenes. In the first, a letter is delivered to the Queen in the presence of the King and the Minister and the Queen leaves the unopened letter on the table in front of everyone. The Minister immediately realizes the incriminating nature of the letter and picks it up off the table, leaving the Queen unable to ask for its return without alerting the King to its importance. The police secretly search for the letter but are unable to find it because they assume that the Minister has hidden it, whereas he has also left the letter on open display in a letter rack hanging from his mantelpiece. In the second scene, we have a repetition of the first, but now the Minister possesses the letter, the police are in the position of not being able to see what is directly under their noses and Dupin is able to see the significance of the now disguised letter openly hanging from the mantelpiece.

Lacan's interpretation of Poe's story focuses upon two main themes: first, the anonymous nature of the letter, which for Lacan serves as the 'true subject' of the story, and, second, the pattern of intersubjective relationships that are repeated in the tale. The reader knows nothing about the letter except that the original script was in a male hand and that it will compromise the Queen if the King knows of its contents. As the letter passes from hand to hand – from Queen to Minister, Minister to Dupin, Dupin to Prefect of Police, Prefect of Police back to Queen – it forms a 'symbolic pact', situating each person who possess it within a chain of symbolic relations. Furthermore, the tale duplicates the relationships between the Queen, King and Minister in the first half of the tale with the relationships between the Minister,

Prefect of Police and Dupin in the second. These rotating positions, or intersubjective relationships, pivot around the shifting position of the letter itself. As the content remains unknown throughout this process of symbolic exchange, we can also say that the letter is a signifier without a signified.

According to Lacan, the various subject positions in the tale can be defined by three distinct forms of 'glance' or 'gaze'. The first glance is the glance that sees nothing, that is to say, the position of the King in the first scene and the police in the second. This, then, can also be seen as the position of the law – the law as blind. The second glance is the glance that 'sees that the first sees nothing and deludes itself as to the secrecy of what it hides' (1988c [1956]: 32). This is the position of the Queen in the first scene and the Minister in the second. The third glance is the glance that 'sees that the first two glances leave what should be hidden exposed to whoever would seize it' (1988c [1956]: 32). This is the position occupied formerly by the Minister and latterly Dupin. We have then a duplicate triangular structure:

King		Police	
L		**L**	
Queen	**Minister**	**Minister**	**Dupin**

For Lacan, *The Purloined Letter* is a precise illustration of his idea that it is the signifier (the letter) that determines the subject. What he is proposing, in fact, is a correlation between the three subject positions he identifies in the story and his three orders or registers: the imaginary, the symbolic and the real, which we can represent thus:

Real	
L	
Imaginary	**Symbolic**

Lacan observes that the King and 'the detectives have so immutable a notion of the real' (1988c [1956]: 39) that they fail to notice what is beneath their very noses. This is what Lacan calls the 'realist's imbecility' or a naive empiricism that thinks that the world is given and we have a direct, unmediated, relationship to it. The second position is that of the seer. In this position the subject sees both that the first position is blind and unaware of what is happening and that the third position is fully aware of what is unfolding and therefore holds the power. But in this position the subject believes that what is hidden (the secrets of the letter) can remain hidden and therefore 'delude' him/herself that it is they who possess the signifier (the letter). In the second position, then, the subject occupies an essentially narcissistic relation to the letter and this corresponds to the imaginary phase we outlined in the previous chapter. The third position is symbolic and in this position the subject 'discerns the role of structure in the situation and acts accordingly' (Muller and Richardson 1988: 63). This is the position of the Minister in the first scene and Dupin in the second. Both figures can see what is taking place in front of them, they understand the implications of the letter, and moreover they know how to act. This is the position of the subject in the symbolic order; a subject who understands their situation within a larger structure and the function of that structure in determining their actions.

First the Queen and then the Minister believe they can possess the letter and keep it hidden. Lacan, however, argues that it is the letter (the signifier) that possesses the subject; it is the signifier that inscribes the subject in the symbolic order. When the Minister takes and hides the letter he readdresses it to himself, but in doing so he changes the masculine script of the original to a feminine one. Thus, suggests Lacan, he is caught up 'in the dynamics of repetition that drag him into the second position' (Muller and Richardson 1988: 63). Similarly, Dupin cannot resist leaving his signature on his own replacement letter and in doing so he is immediately dragged into the second narcissistic position. As Lacan puts it, 'Dupin, from the place he now occupies, cannot help feeling a rage of manifestly feminine nature' (1988c [1956]: 51). In leaving a cryptic message on his letter Dupin is taking revenge on the Minister for a past slight, but at the same time he is giving up his position as a detached analyst or observer. The subject is caught up by the signifier and situated in a chain of signification through a continual process of repetition. 'This is the very effect', writes Lacan, 'of the unconscious in the precise sense we teach that the unconscious means that man is inhabited by the signifier' (1988c [1956]: 48). The subject does not *exist* outside the signifying chain but rather *in-sists* within it. The letter is a floating signifier that passes along the signifying chain with each person unconscious of the full import of what is taking place.

SUMMARY

The 1950s were a period of extraordinary innovation for Lacan. Through the influence of the structural anthropologist Claude Lévi-Strauss and linguists Ferdinand de Saussure and Roman Jakobson, Lacan developed his central notion of the symbolic order and the subject as subject of the signifier. This facilitated Lacan's break with traditional psychoanalysis and paved the way for his major innovation – the idea that the unconscious is structured like a language. In the following chapter we will see what Lacan means by this as well as what distinguishes the Lacanian from the Freudian unconscious and how the emphasis of his work changes from the mid-1960s onwards.

3

THE OEDIPUS COMPLEX
AND THE MEANING
OF THE PHALLUS

In this chapter we will see how Lacan's work moved away from the strict linguistic and Structuralist terminology of the 1950s to elaborate a theory of the subject in terms of unconscious desire and the *drive*. In order to help you understand Lacan's reconceptualization of such psychoanalytic concepts as the phallus, the father and the superego, we will first see how he reformulated the central concept of Freudian psychoanalysis, the Oedipus complex. For Lacan, the phallus is not to be equated with the penis, and as a signifier it performs a different function in each of the three orders: the imaginary, the symbolic and the real. Similarly, the father is a signifier or a metaphor rather than an actual person. As we will see, the 'Name-of-the-Father' is a signifier that breaks the mother/child couple and introduces the child into the symbolic order of desire and lack. Through the function of the father in the Oedipus complex the superego is formed. The superego is the result of the internalization of the father and Lacan had a very innovative understanding of the role of the father and the superego. After giving an account of each of these ideas in turn we will see how the fundamental paradoxicality of psychoanalytic concepts can help us understand social phenomena such as racism and anti-Semitism.

THE OEDIPUS COMPLEX

Freud's conception of the Oedipus complex is probably one of the most popularized and at the same time one of the most misunderstood ideas of psychoanalysis. Taking his cue from the ancient Greek tragedy by Sophocles, *Oedipus Rex*, where Oedipus unwittingly kills his father and becomes king by marrying his mother, Freud suggested that our deepest unconscious desire is to murder our father and marry our mother. The Oedipus complex is rather more complicated than this, though, and represents Freud's attempt to map the ambivalent, both loving and hostile, feelings that the child has towards its parents. In its *positive* form the complex manifests itself as the desire for the death of a rival, the parent of the same sex, accompanied by the sexual desire for the parent of the opposite sex. In its *negative* form the complex works in reverse, as the desire for the parent of the same sex and a hatred towards the parent of the opposite sex. In actual fact, a so-called 'normal' Oedipus complex consists of both positive and negative forms. What is important about the Oedipus complex is how the child learns to negotiate and resolve its ambivalent feelings towards its parents. Freud saw this process as taking place between the ages of three and five years. With the resolution of the Oedipus complex sexuality goes through a period of 'latency' until it reappears during puberty as adolescent sexuality. Most controversially, Freud insisted that the Oedipus complex was a universal, trans-historical and trans-cultural phenomenon:

> [T]he Oedipus complex is the nuclear complex of neuroses, and constitutes the essential part of their content. It represents the peak of infantile sexuality, which, through its after-effects, exercises a decisive influence on the sexuality of adults. Every new arrival on this planet is faced by the task of mastering the Oedipus complex; anyone who fails to do so falls a victim to neurosis.
>
> (Freud 1991d [1905]: 149)

In an early encyclopaedia article on the family (1938) Lacan adopted a fairly orthodox Freudian understanding of the Oedipus complex, and it was not until the 1950s and through the influence of Lévi-Strauss (see Chapter 2) that Lacan began to develop his own distinctive 'structural' model of the complex. For Lacan, the Oedipus complex is primarily a symbolic structure. When two people live together or get married they do so for very personal and intimate reasons, but at the same time there is a wider social or symbolic aspect to this relationship. A relationship or marriage concerns not just the two people involved but also a whole social network of friends, relations and institutions. Thus, personal relationships situate men and women in a symbolic circuit of social meanings. According to Lacan, therefore, we must distinguish between the real people involved and the symbolic structures that organize relationships between men and women. In our society the primary structure that defines our symbolic and unconscious relations is the Oedipus complex. More precisely the Oedipus complex represents a triangular structure that breaks the binary relationship established between the mother and child in the imaginary, although, as we will see, the imaginary is never simply a dual structure – there is always a third element involved. The infant's earliest experiences are characterized by absolute dependence upon the mother as she fulfils the child's needs of feeding, caring and nurturing. At the same time the child is faced with the enigma around the (m)other's desire – What am I in the Other's desire? The answers the child comes up with will be crucial to its resolution of the Oedipus complex.

The Oedipus complex marks the transition from the imaginary to the symbolic. Through the intervention of a third term, the Name-of-the-Father, that closed circuit of mutual desire between the mother and child is broken and a space is created, within which the child can begin to identify itself as a separate being from the mother. Lacan calls this third term the Name-of-the-Father, because it does not have to be the real father, or even a male figure, but is a symbolic position that the child perceives to be the location of the object of the mother's desire. It is also, as we will see, a position of authority and the symbolic law that intervenes to prohibit the child's desire. For Lacan, the key signifier that this whole process turns upon is the *phallus*.

THE MEANING OF THE PHALLUS

According to Freud, the Oedipus complex is contemporaneous with the 'Phallic Phase' of infantile sexuality. Prior to this phase Freud thought of all children as essentially bisexual beings who attained sexual satisfaction through auto-eroticism. By this he means that very young infants gain sexual stimulation through their own bodies. There is no sexual object as such, but they achieve satisfaction through the manipulation of erotogenic zones. An erotogenic zone is any area or organ of the body that is assigned sexual significance by the infant, such as the oral and anal orifices as well as the sexual organs. For example, thumb-sucking is an auto-erotic activity in the sense that it involves the stimulation of a particular area of the body and the infant derives pleasure from it. What changes through the phallic phase is that the genitals become the focus of sexual stimulation. There is a crucial difference, however, between adult and infantile sexuality in that during infancy, for both sexes, 'only one genital, namely the male one, comes into account. What is present, therefore, is not the primacy of the genitals, but the primacy of the *phallus*' (Freud 1991e [1923]: 308). It is the sight of the presence or absence of the penis that forces the child to recognise that boys and girls are different. To begin with, Freud postulated that both sexes disavow the absence of the woman's penis and believe they have seen it, even if it is not there. Eventually, however, they are forced to admit its absence and they account for this absence through the idea of castration. The boy sees the woman as a castrated man and the girl has to accept that she has not got and never will have a penis. Freud did not distinguish between the penis as an actual bodily organ and the 'phallus' as a signifier of sexual difference. The phallus within Freud's work always maintained its reference to the male sexual organ.

For Lacan, the importance of Freud's insight into infantile sexuality was not whether or not girls have a penis and boys fear that theirs will be cut off, but the function of the phallus as a signifier of lack and sexual difference. The phallus in Lacanian theory should not be confused with the male genital organ, although it clearly carries these connotations. The phallus is first and foremost a signifier and in Lacan's system a particularly privileged signifier. The phallus operates in all three of Lacan's registers – the imaginary, the symbolic and the real – and as his system develops it becomes the one single indivisible signifier that anchors the chain of signification. Indeed, it is a particularly privileged signifier, as we will see, because it inaugurates the process of signification itself. In this chapter we will focus on the imaginary and symbolic aspects of the phallus and how these relate through the paternal metaphor to the Name-of-the-Father. We will return to the question of the phallus, jouissance and the real in subsequent chapters.

THE IMAGINARY PHALLUS

As we saw above, the child slowly comes to realise that it is not identical to, or the sole object of, the mother's desire, as her desire is directed elsewhere. He/she will therefore attempt to once again become the object of her desire and return to the initial state of blissful union. The simple dyadic relationship between the mother and child is thus turned into a triangular relationship between the child, the mother and the object of her desire. The child attempts to seduce the mother by becoming that object of desire. Lacan calls this third term the imaginary phallus. The imaginary phallus is what the child *assumes* someone must have in order for them to be the object of the mother's desire and, as her desire is usually directed towards the father, it is assumed that he possesses the phallus. Through trying to satisfy the mother's desire, the child identifies with the object that it presumes she has lost and attempts to become that object for her. The phallus is imaginary in the sense that it is associated in the child's mind with an actual object that has been lost and can be recovered. The Oedipus complex, for Lacan, involves the process of giving up the identification with this imaginary phallus, and recognizing that it is a signifier and as such was never there in the first place. What Freud called castration, therefore, is a symbolic process that involves the infant's recognition of themselves as 'lacking' something – the phallus. For Lacan, castration involves the process whereby boys accept that they can symbolically 'have' the phallus only by accepting that they can never actually have it 'in reality' and girls can accept 'not-having' the phallus once they give up on their 'phallic' identification with their mothers (we will discuss this very complicated idea in more detail in the chapter on sexual difference). This is the function of the Oedipus complex in Lacan.

THE SYMBOLIC PHALLUS

It is through the intervention of the Name-of-the-Father that the imaginary unity between child and mother is broken. The father is assumed to possess something that the child lacks and it is this that the mother desires. It is important here though not to confuse the Name-of-the-Father with the actual father. The Name-of-the-Father is a symbolic function that intrudes into the illusory world of the child and breaks the imaginary dyad of the mother and child. The child assumes that the father is one that satisfies the mother's desire and possesses the phallus. In this sense, argues Lacan, the Oedipus complex involves an element of substitution, that is to say, the substitution of one signifier, the desire of the mother, for another, the Name-of-the-Father. It is through this initial act of substitution that the process of signification begins and child enters the symbolic order as a subject of lack. It is also for this reason that Lacan describes the process of symbolization itself as 'phallic'. It is through the Name-of-the-Father that the phallus is installed as the central organizing signifier of the unconscious. The phallus is the 'original' lost object, but only insofar as no one possessed it in the first place. The phallus, therefore, is not like any other signifier, it is the signifier of absence and does not 'exist' in its own right as a thing, an object or a bodily organ. Let us look at this more closely.

Lacan equates the process of giving up the imaginary phallus with Freud's account of castration anxiety, but he argues that the process of castration in Freud is more complicated than people generally think. Castration involves not just an anxiety about losing one's penis but simultaneously the recognition of *lack* or *absence*. The child is concerned about losing its own penis and simultaneously recognizes that the mother does not have a penis. The idea of the penis, therefore, becomes metonymically linked to the recognition of *lack*. It is in this sense that Lacan argues that the phallus is not simply the penis; it is *the penis plus the recognition of absence or lack*. Castration is not the fear that one has already lost, in the case of girls, or will lose, in the case of boys, one's penis but rather the symbolic process of giving up the idea that one can be the phallus for the mother. The intervention of the father distances the child from the mother and also places the phallus forever beyond its reach. If the symbolic father is seen to possess the phallus, then the child can only become a subject itself in the symbolic order by renouncing the imaginary phallus. The problem for Lacan is how does one symbolically represent 'lack' – something that by definition is not there? His solution is the idea of the 'veil'. The presence of the veil suggests that there is an object behind it, which the veil covers over, although this is only a presumption on the part of the subject. In this way the veil enables the perpetuation of the idea that the object exists. Thus, both boys and girls can have a relationship to the phallus on the basis that it always remains veiled and out of reach. The phallus provides the vital link between desire and signification. It is desire that drives the process of symbolization. The phallus is the ultimate object of desire that we have lost and always search for but never had in the first place.

To summarize, before we explore this complex idea further, the phallus stands for that moment of rupture when the child is forced to recognize the desire of the other; of the mother. 'The mother is refused to the child in so far as a prohibition falls on the child's desire to be what the mother desires' (Rose 1996a: 61). The phallus, therefore, always belongs somewhere else; it breaks the mother/child dyad and initiates the order of symbolic exchange. In this sense the phallus is both imaginary and symbolic. It is imaginary in that it represents the object presumed to satisfy the mother's desire; at the same time, it is symbolic in that it stands in for the recognition that desire cannot be satisfied. By breaking the imaginary couple 'the phallus represents a moment of division [that "lack-in-being"] which re-enacts the fundamental splitting of the subject itself' (Rose 1996a: 63). As a presence in absence, a 'seeming' value, *the phallus is a fraud*.

THE LAW OF THE FATHER AND THE SUPEREGO

It is through the intervention of the father that the child is precipitated out of the imaginary world of infantile plenitude into the symbolic universe of lack. The Oedipus complex marks this transition from imaginary to symbolic, or, as Freud theorized it in such works as *Totem and Taboo* (1991g [1913]) and *Civilisation and its Discontents* (1991f [1930]), the transition from nature to culture. The Oedipus complex for Freud marks the origin of civilization, religion, morals and art. It is only through the repression and sublimation of our incestuous desire for our mothers that civilization and culture can develop. The Lacanian Name-of-the-Father, therefore, is associated with the prohibition of incest and the instigation of symbolic law. The symbolic order and the process of signification, according to Lacan, is 'phallic' and governed by the paternal metaphor and the imposition of paternal law. The father is seen to embody the socio-symbolic law and the function of the paternal metaphor is to substitute the desire for the mother with the law of the father. This is also the founding moment of the unconscious for Lacan and the point at which the phallus is installed as the central organizing signifier of the unconscious. The internalization of the paternal metaphor also creates something else, though, that Freud designates as the *superego*. Lacan has developed the notion of the superego in a very specific and very important way.

The superego emerges through the transition from nature to culture via the internalization of the incest taboo and is often associated with the development of moral conscience. Lacan retains this association between the superego and the law and points to an inherent paradox that Freud did not himself develop. In *Totem and Taboo* Freud argued that the prohibition against incest provided the foundation for all subsequent social laws. In other words, the most fundamental desire of all human subjects is the desire for incest and its prohibition represents the governing principle of all societies. For Lacan, the superego is located in the symbolic order and retains a close but paradoxical relationship to the law. As with the law, the prohibition operates only within the realm of culture and its purpose is always to exclude incest:

> Freud designates the prohibition of incest as the underlying principle of the
> primordial law, the law of which all other cultural developments are no more
> than consequences and ramifications. And at the same time he identifies
> incest as the fundamental desire.
>
> (Lacan 1992 [1986]: 67)

The law, in other words, is founded upon that which it seeks to exclude, or, to put it another way, the desire to break and transgress the law is the very precondition for the existence of the law itself. On the one hand, the superego is a symbolic structure that regulates the subject's desire, and, on the other, there is this senseless, blind imperativeness to it. As Lacan says in seminar XX, nothing forces anyone to enjoy except the superego: 'The superego is the imperative of jouissance – Enjoy!' (1998 [1975]: 3). The superego, therefore, is at once the law and its own destruction or that which undermines the law. The superego emerges at the point where the law – the public or social law – fails and, at this very point of failure, the law is compelled, as Žižek puts it, 'to search for support in an *illegal* enjoyment' (1994: 54). The superego is, in a sense, the dialectical contrary of the public law; it is what Žižek calls its obscene 'nightly' law – that dark underside that always necessarily accompanies the public law. According to psychoanalysis, there is simply no way a subject can avoid this tension between the law and the desire to transgress it and this manifests itself as 'guilt'. Indeed, for psychoanalysis, we are not simply guilty if we break the law and commit incest, but rather we are always-already guilty of the *desire* to commit incest. Hence, the ultimate paradox of the superego: 'the more we submit ourselves to the superego imperative, the greater its pressure, the more we feel guilty' (Žižek 1994: 67). We will see how these ideas work in practice later, but first we need to clarify one final ambiguity regarding the superego.

THE TWO FATHERS

It is through the identification with the Oedipal father that the incest prohibition is internalized and Oedipal desire abandoned and it is this process, for Freud, that constitutes the superego. But what we find here in Freud is not one notion of the father but *two*. There is first of all the father of the Oedipus complex, who intervenes and disrupts the relationship between mother and child and thus denies the child's access to the mother's desire. This is the father who transmits the law to the child – the law of the incest prohibition – and subordinates the child's desire to the law. It is important to keep in mind, though, that this father is himself subject to the law. Second, there is the primal father of *Totem and Taboo*, who is perceived to be outside the law. In Freud's myth of origins the primal father is a figure of absolute power; the father who aggregates to himself the women and wealth of the primal horde by expelling his sons and rivals. What distinguishes this tyrannical figure from the Oedipal father is that he is not himself subordinated to the law – the law that prohibits his son's access to the women of the horde. This other father, therefore – the cruel and licentious one – is the reverse side of the law. Both fathers function psychically at the level of the superego.

Identification with the primal father involves an ambiguous process whereby the subject simultaneously identifies with authority, the law *and*, at the same time, the illicit desires that would transgress and undermine the law. As with the notion of the superego itself, the father functions in a peculiarly paradoxical way. He is simultaneously the agency of authority and a figure outside the law who actively transgresses the law that he imposes upon others. The subject, therefore, is faced with its subordination to authority and the regulation of its desires through the internalization of a signifier that is itself beyond the law. At a psychic level, an overly punishing superego and subordination to the symbolic law is one way in which the subject comes to resolve this unbearable situation. And yet, by implication, if one must exert strong measures to prohibit something, there must be a correspondingly strong desire to commit the crime. Let us now see how this vicious cycle of transgression and punishment operates in the social domain through Žižek's analysis of racism and anti-Semitism.

RACISM, ANTI-SEMITISM AND THE IMPERATIVE TO ENJOYMENT!

Racism and anti-Semitism are both social and psychic structures. Here I will focus upon the unconscious, psychic, aspect of these processes, but this should not be taken to imply that we can reduce either to psychological explanations alone. More specifically we will see how racism and anti-Semitism are exemplary of the superegoic structures we have considered above. Both racism and anti-Semitism are inherently contradictory ideologies. In the UK for example, we constantly hear and read in the media that immigrants are 'flooding' the country in order to freeload on our welfare state. At the same time, these very same immigrants are attacked for stealing our jobs and therefore putting ordinary citizens out of work. There is clearly a contradiction here – if immigrants are living a life of luxury on state benefits then they are not working; if on the other hand, they are working hard and taking our jobs, then they are clearly not living off the state but contributing to it. What psychoanalysis adds to our understanding of this process is how subjects manage to sustain these contradictory beliefs.

The relationship between racism and anti-Semitism is a complex and changing one. Žižek observes that traditionally anti-Semitism has always been considered as an 'exception' and conceptualized differently to other forms of racism. Whereas classical racism propounds an ideology of national superiority, whereby so-called 'inferior' races were enslaved, anti-Semitism involves the systematic and organized annihilation of the Jewish people. Moreover, Nazi propaganda linked the need for genocide to another fundamental element of its ideology. It was not just that the Jews had to be killed because they represented a threat to the state, but more importantly that the socio-symbolic order itself – the new Aryan state – could not be fully realized without that process taking place; and it is here that the notion of the superego comes into play.

The 'Jew', or the Jewish race, is presented within fascist propaganda as a figure who transgresses and undermines the law and as such must be first punished and eventually eradicated so that a new harmonious Aryan society can emerge. Furthermore, the Nazis claimed that, because there were so many Jewish people who occupied positions of wealth and power, then the state must be strong and authoritative to counteract them. On the one hand, therefore, we find in fascist propaganda the portrayal of Jewish people as less than human – as insects and rodents – so that it is easier to rationally justify their extermination and, on the other, the attribution to them of excessive power and influence. That is to say, a dual process is taking place whereby the dehumanizing of the other is accompanied by an inflation of the other's power and strength. If a particular group is so small and insignificant that we can simply stamp them out then why bother? They cannot pose that much of a threat. We must eradicate the other precisely because they are rich, powerful and influential. But, more importantly, by being rich, powerful and influential they are depriving *us* of our rightful position in society. What we find in anti-Semitism is that vicious cycle articulated through the superego, whereby the law – the prohibition that maintains and regulates the social order – draws its strength from that which it excludes. The more authoritarian a regime becomes the greater the threat against it must be *presumed* to be. Nazi ideology, therefore, involves a particular fantasy structure (see Chapter 5 for an account of fantasy) that allows the subject to reconcile the apparently contradictory positions that the Jewish people are at once less than human and as such represent an insidious threat to 'our way of life' and at the same time are superhuman, hence their greater power, influence and success. Let me elaborate this notion of a dual fantasy a little further.

According to psychoanalysis, there is always a good and a bad side to fantasy. There is the blissful dream state beyond the mundane aspects of our lives and the horrors of modern civilization, but this is always accompanied by a darker side that involves envy, irritation and malice. Totalitarianism provides a perfect illustration of this dual structure. First, there is the utopian side – the fantasy of the perfect state as a unified harmonious community of organically, naturally, linked people. This utopianism, however, is always accompanied by its opposite – those fantasies of plots, conspiracies and threats that stop the realization of this utopia. Thus, argues Žižek, insofar as a community experiences its reality as regulated and harmoniously structured, it has to repress the inherent conflict at its very heart. In other words, for a utopian fantasy to work, it presupposes the disavowal and repression of part of itself, and its effectiveness depends on how well it does this. For the Nazis, the Jews performed precisely this function. The figure of 'the Jew' is the precondition for anti-Semitic ideology; it is that which sustains anti-Semitism. What Žižek calls the 'conceptual Jew' must be invented and sustained at the level of fantasy for anti-Semitic ideology to work. Interestingly, argues Žižek, Nazi ideology was often most virulent in those areas of Germany that had the fewest Jews. Paradoxically, then, the smaller the threat and the actual number of Jews present, the greater their power was perceived to be. This in turn, of course, legitimates a greater use of repression and force, which in turn presupposes a stronger threat against it. This is the vicious, self-punishing, cycle of the superego.

There is also something else taking place here, though. For any authoritarian regime to exist, however totalitarian it may be, the active participation and support of a population is required, otherwise the regime will very quickly collapse. And yet, why would any population support an overtly repressive regime? This is where the ambiguity of the father and what Lacan calls the superegoic imperative to Enjoy comes in. When a subject identifies with a leader/father figure, he/she identifies with a position of Oedipal power and authority. At the same time, however, the subject identifies with that cruel and licentious father of the primal horde. If we do not have access to pleasure and enjoyment, we assume that it is because someone else has usurped our position and taken it from us. Hence, the inflated images of power and potency ascribed to other 'minority' groups. According to Žižek, this is the logic that is at work in anti-Semitism. The efficacy of the figure of the 'Jew' relies on the assumption of a certain surplus – that Jews possess something that we do not and therefore they have access to pleasures that we are denied. For racism and anti-Semitism to function psychically an impossible, unfathomable enjoyment, allegedly stolen from us, must be attributed to the other. Paradoxically, argues Žižek, what 'holds together' a given community is

> not so much identification with the public or symbolic Law that regulates the community's 'normal' everyday life, but rather *identification with a specific form of transgression of the Law, of the Law's suspension* (in psychoanalytic terms, with a specific form of *enjoyment*).
>
> (1994: 55)

More specifically, what holds communities together is the attribution of *excessive* enjoyment to other or alien groups; for instance, the stereotypical fantasy of sexual potency associated with black men. This attribution of excessive enjoyment to the other then comes to operate as a specific form of theft for the subject – the theft of one's own enjoyment.

Psychoanalysis argues that the inherent ambiguity of these psychic structures – the superego, the father and fantasy – is a necessary and constitutive part of all social orders and essential to their proper functioning. If the threat is not actually, empirically, there then it will have to be invented, just as Nazi ideology had to construct the 'conceptual Jew' in order to justify its own repressive regime. The point is that the Jew is not the cause of that ideology, but rather something that is constituted in its effects, that is to say, the Jew is posited retrospectively as the condition of possibility for the fascist regime. The notion of the 'conceptual Jew' is what gives the irrationality of fascist ideology its coherence and consistency. Within racism and anti-Semitism, enjoyment, and specifically an 'excess' of enjoyment, is always imputed to the other: 'the other may be lazy but they still have more fun than us; they live off our hard work etc.'. However, that is not enough in itself for racism to take hold. The enjoyment of the other must also be seen as depriving us of our own enjoyment: 'we work hard to build a community we can be proud of and be happy within, but this goal is denied us by lazy scrounging foreigners. We can therefore not enjoy our community because they have stolen away from us that which would most fully realize our enjoyment.' This is what Žižek sees as the logic of racism and anti-Semitism: *the theft of enjoyment*.

SUMMARY

Lacan reformulated the central complex of psychoanalysis, the Oedipus complex, as a *symbolic structure*. Thus, for Lacan, the threat of castration does not involve an actual bodily threat but a symbolic process, as the infant assumes a position in the symbolic order as a desiring subject. Similarly, Lacan radically reformulated the role of the father. The role of the father in psychoanalysis depends not upon the presence of an actual father but upon a signifier, the paternal metaphor, which substitutes the desire of the mother with symbolic law. It is through the intervention of the Name-of-the-Father that the dyadic relationship of the imaginary is broken and the phallus is installed as the original lost object. The phallus is the original object-cause of desire and the central organizing signifier of the unconscious. These ideas are linked through the notion of the two fathers to the function of the superego, as at once the internalization of the symbolic law and the desire to transgress this law. In the following chapter we will look more closely at the question of desire and the subject of the unconscious.

4

THE SUBJECT OF THE UNCONSCIOUS

In the previous two chapters we focused on Lacan's work from the 1950s, when he placed the greatest emphasis on the role of language and the symbolic order. Lacan was *not* a Structuralist in any strict sense of the term, however, for two reasons. First, Structuralism sought to dissolve the subject completely and saw subjects as merely the 'effect' of symbolic structures. Lacan, on the other hand, while seeking to locate the constitution of the subject in relation to the symbolic, does not see the subject as simply reducible to an effect of language or the symbolic order. Second, for Structuralism, a structure is always complete, while for Lacan the structure – the symbolic order – is never complete. There is always something left over; an excess or something that exceeds the symbolic. What exceeds the symbolic is the subject and the object.

In this chapter we will look at this exception in terms of the subject and in the following chapter in relation to the *objet petit a*. In seminar XI (1964) an important break was introduced into Lacan's work, as he sought to distinguish his own conception of the unconscious from Freud's and more systematically formulate what is *beyond* language and structure. He also replaced the linguistic categories of metaphor and metonymy with the new concepts of *alienation* and *separation*. As we will see, the processes of alienation and separation are closely linked to the psychoanalytic conception of desire and the drive, and in order to help you understand these difficult concepts we will look at Lacan's reading of Shakespeare's *Hamlet*.

FORMATIONS OF THE UNCONSCIOUS

The unconscious for Freud is essentially *representation*, in the sense that it consists of the memory traces of early infantile experiences and traumas. Throughout his career Freud developed a number of different models of the mind: the economic or dynamic model of powerful desires originating in the unconscious and seeking expression in consciousness; the topographical model of the conscious, pre-conscious and unconscious; and finally the structural model of the id, ego and superego (see Thurschwell (2000: ch. 5) for an account of these different models). Similarly, Lacan developed a number of different definitions of the unconscious and the emphasis that he placed on each conceptualization changed throughout his career. We will consider three specific definitions of the unconscious advanced by Lacan below:

* The unconscious as a gap or rupture.
* The unconscious as structured like a language.
* The unconscious as the discourse of the Other.

First, let us consider what we mean by the unconscious.

According to Lacan, psychoanalysis is a science. It is the science of the unconscious subject, and this subject first emerged in the seventeenth century with the founder of modern philosophy René Descartes (1596–1650). Lacan interprets the Freudian unconscious as both the direct heir of the Cartesian subject and, at the same time, that which undermines all philosophies deriving from it. In *Meditations* (1642) Descartes asked how we might know the truth of our beliefs and our perceptions of reality. He suggested that we could only do this scientifically if we rejected everything that we had cause to doubt and then saw what remained with certainty as true. The difficulty with this approach, Descartes observed, is that it could lead one into more difficulties and uncertainty than the position from which one originally started. One would have to accept, as Descartes put it, that 'there was nothing at all in the world: no sky, no earth, no minds or bodies' (1968 [1642]: 103). Descartes concluded, then, that all we could be certain of was the existence of God and ourselves:

> There is therefore no doubt that I exist, if he [God] deceives me; and let him
> deceive me as much as he likes, he can never cause me to be nothing, so long
> as I think I am something. So that, after having thought carefully about it, and
> having scrupulously examined everything, one must then, in conclusion, take
> as assured that the proposition: *I am*, *I exist*, is necessarily true, everytime I
> express it or conceive of it in my mind.

(1968 [1642]: 103)

From a Lacanian perspective, on the other hand, as Slavoj Žižek puts it, the only thing one can be certain of is that *one does not exist*. Let us try to clarify this. Freud remains Cartesian to the extent that he sets out from a position of doubt, but, whereas Descartes moves from a position of doubt to the certainty of conscious mind, Freud moves in the opposite direction and places the emphasis on the *doubt* that supports certainty. For Freud, it is the central tenet of psychoanalysis that the vast majority of mental life and activity remains inaccessible to the conscious mind. He famously used the image of an iceberg to illustrate the human mind, in the sense that only a fraction of an iceberg is immediately visible and the majority of it remains submerged beneath the surface. Lacan argues that if we take the Freudian unconscious seriously then we must reverse Descartes' formulation thus: '*By virtue of the fact that I doubt, I am sure that I think*' (1979 [1973]: 35). The certainty of consciousness is always supported by something else: by doubt, by the unknown or unknowable, or by what Freud will designate as the unconscious. For Lacan, therefore, the only thing we can know with certainty after Freud is 'that the subject of the unconscious manifests itself, that it thinks before it attains certainty' (1979 [1973]: 37). In this sense the unconscious is pre-ontological; it is not a question of existence, of being or non-being, but rather of the *unrealized*, the unknown of Cartesian doubt. We must be quite clear here though that the unconscious is not the act of doubting as such, as this presupposes an already existing subject. The unconscious is the unknown that lies beyond doubt.

THE UNCONSCIOUS AS GAP OR RUPTURE

The unconscious, writes Lacan, must 'be apprehended in its experience of rupture, between perception and consciousness, in that non-temporal locus, . . . Freud calls . . . another scene' (1979 [1973]: 56).

According to Freud we know that there is an unconscious because it manifests itself at precisely those moments when our conscious defence mechanisms are at their weakest; for example, through our dreams when we sleep, in those accidental slips of the tongue when we say something that we did not really intend to say but we often mean, through jokes which frequently reveal more about us than we think, or, finally, through the symptoms of mental distress and illness. What each of these examples points to, argued Freud, is the presence of processes beyond conscious thought that erupt and disrupt everyday speech and experience. This is the Freud of the early texts on language: *The Interpretation of Dreams* (1991a [1900]), *The Psychopathology of Everyday Life* (1991b [1901]) and *Jokes and Their Relation to the Unconscious* (1991c [1905]). In seminar XI Lacan remains very close to these texts, defining the unconscious in terms of 'impediment', 'failure' and 'splitting'. The unconscious manifests itself at those points when language fails and stumbles. The unconscious *is* precisely this gap or rupture in the symbolic chain. So in what sense can Lacan also say that the unconscious is structured like a language?

THE UNCONSCIOUS IS STRUCTURED LIKE A LANGUAGE

That the unconscious is structured like a language is Lacan's central thesis and probably his most influential contribution to psychoanalysis as well as literary and cultural studies. Freud described the unconscious as a realm without syntax or grammar; a realm without temporality or contradiction. Does this not directly contradict Lacan's thesis? For Freud, all mental states are either ideas (representations) or ideas plus affect (energy) and in this respect he distinguished between 'word-presentations' – the product of the secondary processes of conscious thought – and 'thing-presentations' – the product of the primary processes of the unconscious. These are very complicated ideas in Freud and he never explicitly spelt out what he meant by them. Many critics have taken Freud's distinction between the primary and secondary processes to mean that conscious thought is concerned with language while the unconscious is concerned with images and feelings. Lacan is completely against this idea.

The unconscious, according to Lacan, is governed by the rules of the signifier as it is language that translates sensory images into structure. We can only know the unconscious through speech and language; therefore, similar kinds of relationships exist between unconscious elements, signifiers and other forms of language. As we saw in the previous chapter, the unconscious is constituted through the subject's articulation in the symbolic order. The Lacanian unconscious is not an individual unconscious, in the sense that Freud speaks of *the* unconscious; neither is it a *collective* unconscious in the sense that Carl Gustave Jung (1875–1961) defines it, that is, as a repository or reservoir of mythical images (archetypes) and racial inheritance. The Lacanian unconscious is rather the *effect* of a trans-individual symbolic order upon the subject. We can draw from this three related theses:

1 The unconscious is not biological but is something that *signifies*.
2 The unconscious is the effect – the impact – upon the subject of the trans-individual symbolic order.
3 The unconscious is structured like a language.

Fink argues that the Lacanian unconscious is not only structured *like* a language but *is* language, insofar as it is language that makes up the unconscious. This involves us in rethinking, however, what we mean by language. Language, for Lacan, designates not simply verbal speech or written text but any signifying system that is based upon differential relations. The unconscious is structured like a language in the sense that it is a signifying process that involves coding and decoding, or ciphering and deciphering. The unconscious comes into being in the symbolic order in the *gap* between signifier and signified, through the sliding of the signified beneath the signifier and the failure of meaning to be fixed (see Chapter 2). In short, the unconscious is something that signifies and must be deciphered.

In seminar XX Lacan formulated this distinction between his own use of the term 'language' and linguistics through the neologism *la linguisterie*. Linguistics is concerned with the formalization of language and knowledge. *La linguisterie* on the other hand is the side of language that linguistics ignores. It refers to those points in language when meaning fails and breaks down; it is the science of the word that fails. Fink rather nicely translates *la linguisterie* as 'linguistricks', which serves to emphasize the playfulness of the unconscious and the way it is always trying to trip the subject up, playing tricks on conscious thought. It is in this sense and not in the sense of formal linguistics that the unconscious is structured like a language. Let us now turn to Lacan's third definition of the unconscious as the discourse of the Other.

THE UNCONSCIOUS IS THE DISCOURSE OF THE OTHER

Freud spoke of the unconscious as '(an)other scene' – the immutable realm of human desire. Lacan speaks of the unconscious as quite simply the 'discourse of the Other' (1977e [1960]). There is an important distinction being made here by Lacan between the little other and the capitalized big Other. The lower case 'other' always refers to imaginary others. We treat these others as whole, unified or coherent egos, and as reflections of ourselves they give us the sense of being complete whole beings. This is the other of the mirror phase who the infant presumes will completely satisfy its desire. At the same time the infant sees itself as the sole object of desire for the other (see Chapter 1). The big Other, on the other hand, is that absolute otherness that we cannot assimilate to our subjectivity. The big Other is the symbolic order; it is that foreign language that we are born into and must learn to speak if we are to articulate our own desire. It is also the discourse and desires of those around us, through which we internalize and inflect our own desire. What psychoanalysis teaches us is that our desires are always inextricably bound up with the desires of others. In the first instance these are the desires of our parents, as they place upon the newborn infant all their hopes and wishes for a prosperous and fulfilled life, but also in the sense that they invest in their children all their own unfilled dreams and aspirations. These unconscious desires and wishes of others flow into us through language – through discourse – and therefore desire is always shaped and moulded by language. We can only express our desire through the language we have and we must learn that language through others. According to Lacan, just as there is no such thing as the unconscious without language, it is through language that desire comes into being. Unconscious desire, therefore, emerges in relation to the big Other – the symbolic order. It is the *discourse of the Other*, insofar as we are condemned to speak our desire through the language and desires of others. As Fink writes, 'we can say that the unconscious is full of such foreign desires' (1995: 9).

The psychoanalytic subject – the subject of the unconscious – can only come into being through others and in relation to the Other. As Lacan puts it, the subject unfolds in the place (locus) of the Other. As with the Cartesian subject, the subject of the unconscious is faced with the question of its own existence, or, more precisely, its lack of existence. Unlike the Cartesian subject, however, the Lacanian subject does not have the certainty of self-consciousness – *I think, therefore, I am*; the Lacanian subject of the unconscious is essentially *no-thing*; it is a lacking subject who has lost his or her being. The subject in Lacan can also be seen to have a certain equivalence to the unconscious and desire, and these three concepts emerge at the same point within Lacanian theory. The question psychoanalysis poses is: how can something come of nothing? In the 1950s Lacan suggested that the subject was the effect of signifiers and was realized through the processes of metaphor and metonymy. In seminar XI he substituted for metaphor and metonymy the operations of *alienation* and *separation*. These two operations describe the process by which the subject realizes him or herself in the Other.

ALIENATION AND SEPARATION

Alienation designates the process through which the subject first identifies with the signifier and is thereafter determined by the signifier. This is essentially the subject of speech and language that preoccupied Lacan for the first ten years of his seminar. In the 1950s Lacan described two moments of alienation and suggested that the subject was doubly alienated: first, through the infant's (mis)-recognition of itself in the other during the mirror stage and, second, through the subject's accession into the symbolic and language. Alienation is an inevitable consequence of the formation of the ego and a necessary first step towards subjectivity. Contrary to the usual understanding of the term in philosophy or political theory – that is, alienation as *self*-alienation that must be overcome if the true self is to emerge – alienation, for Lacan, is unavoidable and untranscendable. The alienated subject is the subject of the signifier; it is the subject that is determined by the symbolic order and language and is constitutively split or divided. From the mid-1960s onwards Lacan no longer spoke of these two moments of alienation but elaborated a single process that designates the subject's determination by the signifier. From a Lacanian perspective 'alienation is destiny' (Soler 1995a: 49) – we cannot escape language and language inscribes us in a certain position within the symbolic.

Lacan's breakthrough in seminar XI was the introduction of the concept of 'separation'. Separation is linked to desire and designates the process through which the child differentiates itself from the (m)Other and is not simply a subject of language. It is through the concept of separation that we can see that a frequent criticism of Lacan – that he reduces everything to language – is based on a very partial reading of his early seminars. Separation takes place in the domain of desire and requires from the subject a certain 'want to be'; a 'want to be' separate from the signifying chain. It also involves a 'want to know' of that which is outside structure, and beyond language and the Other. However, the Other in this case is not the same as the Other of alienation. Previously we considered the Other as consisting of signifiers, but the Other of separation is first and foremost a 'lacking' Other. We will see what Lacan means by this below, but first let us consider what we mean by *desire*.

Lacan is very careful to distinguish between a 'need' and 'desire'. A need such as hunger or thirst can be satisfied. Desire on the other hand refers to something beyond basic human needs that cannot be satisfied. For Lacan, desire is a much broader and more abstract concept than either libido or 'wish' in Freud; in seminar XI he describes it, following Spinoza, as '*the essence of man*' (1979 [1973]: 275). Desire is at the very core of our being and as such it is essentially a relation to *lack*; indeed, desire and lack are inextricably tied together. Lacan defines desire as the remainder that arises from the subtraction of *need* from *demand*:

> Thus desire is neither the appetite for satisfaction, nor the demand for love, but the difference that results from the subtraction of the first from the second, the phenomenon of their splitting (*Spaltung*).

> (1977d [1958]: 287)

Desire and the unconscious are founded through the recognition of a fundamental lack: the absence of the phallus. Desire, therefore, is always the manifestation of something that is lacking in the subject and the Other – the symbolic order. It is through the Other that the subject secures its position in the symbolic, social, order. The Other confers upon the subject its symbolic mandate, as it is through the desire of the Other that the subject's own desire is founded:

> In the child's attempt to grasp what remains essentially indecipherable in the Other's desire – what Lacan calls the X, the variable, or (better) the unknown – the child's own desire is founded; the Other's desire begins to function as the cause of the child's desire.
>
> (Fink 1995: 59)

The infant's earliest experiences are characterized by an absolute dependence upon the (m)Other, as she fulfils the child's needs of feeding, caring and nurturing. In this scenario the infant fantasizes that the (m)Other can fulfil all its needs and desires and, as it is the centre of attention, the infant assumes that it equally fulfils the mother's desire. Gradually, the infant realizes that the mother is not as dependent upon it as he/she is upon her and that a part of her desire is directed elsewhere. Faced with this dilemma Lacan suggests that the child poses a series of questions to itself: what does she want from me? What am I for her? What does she desire? The infant is forced to recognize that not only is he/she a split and lacking subject but also that the (m)Other is a desiring subject and therefore lacking something. The (m)Other is never perfect and the infant's demand for love goes *beyond* the objects that satisfy its needs. For Lacan it is this irreducible 'beyond' of the demand that constitutes desire.

As with the subject the Other is also lacking; the Other is also 'barred'. There remains something essentially unfathomable in the desire of the Other for the subject. What Lacan calls separation is this encounter with the lack in the Other and the 'want to be', more than merely lack. Separation involves the coincidence, or overlapping, of two lacks: the lack in the subject and the Other. The interaction between these two lacks will determine the constitution of the subject. Separation, therefore, takes place at precisely the point that the subject can formulate the question: what am I in the Other's desire? and can thus differentiate itself from the desire of the Other. While the desire of the Other always exceeds or escapes the subject, there nevertheless remains something that the subject can recover and thus sustain 'him or herself in being, as a *being of desire*' (Fink 1995: 61), or a desiring subject. That remainder is the *objet petit a*, the object-cause of desire (see Chapter 5).

THE LACANIAN SUBJECT

The Lacanian subject is, therefore, constituted through two movements: the first corresponds to the process of alienation through
language, the second to the separation of desire. Lacan never, however,
precisely designates the point at which the subject appears, because it
never appears as such. The subject in Lacanian psychoanalysis has
no permanence or persistence. Lacan always refers to the subject as
arriving or having just arrived; as always too early or too late. There
is never a point in time that the subject can be said to finally emerge
as a stable and complete entity. It emerges only fleetingly through a
continuous process of subjectification – alienation and separation –
rather than at a specific moment in time. Paul Verhaeghe summarizes
the process well:

> [T]he subject, confronted with the enigma of the desire of the Other, tries to
> verbalise this desire and thus constitutes itself by identifying with the signi-
> fiers in the field of the Other, without ever succeeding in filling the gap
> between subject and Other. Hence, the continuous movement from signifier to
> signifier, in which the subject alternately appears and disappears.
>
> (1998: 168)

What is crucial here is that the subject *assumes* its position within the
symbolic order and is thus able to act. The subject is not simply determined by structure. To become a subject, one must take a position in
relation to the desire of the Other. The infant must differentiate itself
from the desire of the Other. It is this element of choice that allows
for the possibility of change, beyond the inescapable determination of
the symbolic. Lacan referred to this as the 'future anterior' – the future
past. The subject makes a choice that will determine its future but,
paradoxically, this is grounded on the indeterminateness of the unconscious and desire. The subject is, in a sense, suspended between a
'subject-to-be' and the field of the Other, in a continuous vacillation
or fading but never substantively present. But if the subject has no
permanence or consistency and it is not merely the effect of language
or discourse, what is it? What is there beyond language and the
symbolic that makes the subject more than the subject of the signifier?
The answer to this absolutely fundamental question is to be found in
the psychoanalytic understanding of the *drive*. There is no subject
distinct from the drive.

THE DRIVE

Freud's theory of the drive was revised extensively throughout his career. The drive, or instinct as it is usually translated in English, is a concept that exists on the border between the somatic (bodily) and the mental. It consists of a quantity of energy and its psychical representative (remember what we said above about the unconscious being representation). Jean Laplanche and Serge Leclaire define the Freudian drive as 'a constant force of a biological nature, emanating from organic sources, that always has as its aim its own satisfaction through the elimination of the state of tension which operates at the source of the drive itself' (1972 [1965]: 140). According to Freud, there are four characteristics of the drive: its 'pressure', its 'aim', its 'object' and its 'source' (1984c [1915]: 118). By pressure Freud means the drive's motor factor, that is to say, 'the amount of force or measure of the demand for work which it represents' (1984c [1915]: 118). Exerting pressure is a characteristic common to all drives and represents the drive's essence. The aim of the drive is to seek its own satisfaction and it achieves this by removing the source of stimulation. The object of the drive is that which the drive attaches itself to in order to achieve its aim. Freud designates a particularly close attachment between the drive and its object as 'fixation'. Finally, the source of the drive is 'the somatic process which occurs in an organ or part of the body and whose stimulus is represented in mental life by an instinct' (1984c [1915]: 119). The drive, in short, is something that originates within the body and seeks expression in the psyche as representation. Freud is primarily concerned with the aims of the drives and how they seek satisfaction.

We cannot go into Freud's different theories of the drive in detail here, but it is crucial to acknowledge the distinction between an instinct and a drive. An instinct designates a need that can be satisfied. The examples Freud usually gives are the ones I used above – those of hunger and thirst. These needs give rise to an excitation within the body that can be satisfied and neutralized. The drive, on the other hand, cannot be satisfied and is characterized by the *constancy* of the pressure it exerts on consciousness. The model of the Freudian drive is *libido* – sexual energy – or what is also translated as 'wish' or 'desire'. According to Laplanche and Leclaire, it is the introduction of the drive into the sphere of need that marks the distinction between a need and desire: 'the drive introduces into the sphere of need an erotic quality: libido will be substituted for need' (1972 [1965]: 140). Libido is the fundamental motive force of human beings; it is unconscious desire which is the organizing principle of all human thought, action and social relations. Throughout his career Freud maintained a dualistic theory of drives. In the *Project for a Scientific Psychology* (1954 [1895]) he distinguished between bound and unbound energy. In *Three Essays on the Theory of Sexuality* (1991d [1905]) Freud distinguished between libido and the ego-instincts, or the drive to self-preservation. Finally, when he came to accept the criticisms of his fellow analysts that the drive to self-preservation was also sexual in nature, he formulated his final great mythopoetic theory of Eros, the pleasure principle, and Thanatos, the death drive, in *Beyond the Pleasure Principle* (1984b [1920]).

For Lacan, the Freudian notion of the drive is probably the single most important contribution of psychoanalysis to the field of human psychology and our understanding of subjectivity. Lacan insisted on the need to retain the Freudian distinction between the drive and instinct, and in his early work the drive is closely associated with desire. Above all, the drive shares with desire the property of never achieving its aim. The drive always circles around its object but never achieves the satisfaction of reaching it. The purpose of the drive, therefore, is simply to maintain its own repetitive compulsive movement, just as the purpose of desire is to desire. Lacan's theory of the drive, however, differed from Freud's in two important respects. Freud argued that sexuality was composed of a series of partial drives which he defined as the oral, anal and phallic phases. These phases become integrated into a single, whole, genital drive after the resolution of the Oedipus complex. Contrary to Freud, Lacan argues that all drives are partial in the sense that there is never a single integrated harmonious resolution of the drives in the subject. Furthermore, a partial drive does not represent a *part of* a singular unified drive, but rather the *partiality* of the drive in the reproduction of sexuality (see Chapter 6). Lacan also developed Freud's theory of the drive in another important respect. He thought that it was important to retain Freud's dualism, rather than reducing everything to a single motivating force, but rejected Freud's notion of two distinct drives, Eros and Thanatos. For Lacan every drive is sexual in nature and at the same time every drive is a death drive. There is fundamentally only one drive for Lacan – the death drive – and as we will see this drive will increasingly be associated with the real and *jouissance*. From seminar XI onwards Lacan will oppose the drive and jouissance to desire, and that little piece of the real – of jouissance – that the subject has access to will be designated the *objet petit a* (see Chapter 5). These are very difficult ideas and, in order to help you understand them better, let us look at Lacan's conception of the subject in relation to the desire of the Other through his reading of Shakespeare's *Hamlet*.

HAMLET AND THE TRAGEDY OF DESIRE

Along with Sophocles' *Oedipus Rex*, *Hamlet* has been a central literary reference for psychoanalysis. In the *Interpretation of Dreams*, Freud produced the first piece of psychoanalytic literary criticism, when he distinguished between the two plays on the basis of the secular advance of repression in the emotional life of humanity:

> In the *Oedipus* the child's wishful phantasy that underlies it is brought into the open and realised as it would be in a dream. In *Hamlet* it remains repressed; and – just as in the case of neurosis – we only learn of its existence from its inhibiting consequences. Strangely enough, the overwhelming effect produced by the more modern tragedy has turned out to be compatible with the fact that people have remained completely in the dark as to the hero's character.
>
> (Freud 1991a [1900]: 366–7)

For Freud, and later for Ernest Jones (1949), Hamlet's hesitation to act and revenge the death of his father at the hands of his uncle could be explained in terms of his repressed Oedipal desire for his mother. By killing Hamlet's father and then marrying his mother, his uncle had fulfilled Hamlet's own unconscious wish and therefore Hamlet was unable to kill him in turn. For Lacan, on the other hand, *Hamlet* is not a play about repressed Oedipal scenarios, but rather a drama of subjectivity and desire (1982). *Hamlet* is a tragedy of desire; the tragedy of a man who has lost the way of his desire as it is inextricably tied up with the desire of the Other. As Elizabeth Wright writes, Lacan uses *Hamlet* 'as an allegory both of blocked desire and the act of mourning which unlocks it' (1999: 77). In 'Mourning and Melancholia' (1917) Freud suggested that the work of mourning involved the gradual withdrawal of libido from a loved one who had died. This process takes place slowly and, in the meantime, 'the existence of the lost object [person] is psychically prolonged' (1984d [1917]: 253) and the subject's desire remains fixed on the lost object. Once the work of mourning is complete the subject is free to direct their desire elsewhere. According to Lacan, Hamlet was unable fully to mourn his dead father because his mother prematurely married his uncle and replaced the symbolic father. The mother, therefore, replaced the lost object with a new one before Hamlet could withdraw his desire and direct it elsewhere. As we saw in the previous chapter, the original lost object is the phallus and what Lacan is suggesting is that Hamlet is unable to mourn the loss of the phallus that will inaugurate the movement of his own desire. In this situation Freud suggested that mourning turns into melancholia. The crucial difference between mourning and melancholia is that in the act of 'mourning it is the world which has become poor and empty; in melancholia it is the ego itself' (Freud 1984d [1917]: 254). In melancholia the act of mourning is narcissistically turned back upon the self and the subject identifies his/her own ego with the lost object. Melancholia, therefore, has the effect of blocking the natural process of mourning and freezing the subject in time.

Lacan associates narcissism with the imaginary order (see Chapter 1) and the mother/child dyad. The dilemma for Hamlet, argues Lacan, is how to separate himself from the demand of the (m)Other and realize his own desire. Lacan, therefore, interprets Hamlet's notorious hesitation to act and revenge the death of his father as a manifestation of the desire of the Other. Hamlet simply cannot choose between his own desire and the desire of the Other. We need to be clear here though that it is not Hamlet's desire *for* his mother that inhibits him, but his fixation *within* his mother's desire. Hamlet is simply unable to differentiate his own desire from his mother's desire. Hamlet confuses and distorts his own desire; he sees his desire not as constituted in relation to the Other but as the same as the Other.

This confusion can also be seen through Hamlet's relationship with Ophelia. Lacan reads Ophelia as the object of desire – the *objet petit a*, or object-cause of Hamlet's desire. At the beginning of the play Hamlet is estranged from Ophelia. He distances himself from her, from the loved object, but in doing so he dissolves the imaginary relations between subject and object. By dissolving the boundary between subject and object Hamlet is unable to realize his own subjectivity. His whole being is consumed with the rejection of the object of desire and thus, paradoxically, he is trapped within the desire of the Other.

Ophelia can only become the object of his desire once more when she is dead, that is to say, when she is once again unattainable. For Lacan, the tragedy of Hamlet is the tragedy of a subject who is suspended within the time of the Other. Hamlet always acts too early (as with the killing of Polonius) or too late (as with his failure to kill Claudius in the church or recognize his object of desire) until the final hour. It is only at the very end of the play, when Hamlet himself is mortally wounded, that he assumes his position as a subject.

SUMMARY

According to Lacan we cannot know what *the* unconscious *is*. Indeed, it is not a thing as such but a hypothesis; we cannot know the unconscious, but only deduce it from a subject's speech. We can deduce that there is 'knowledge', an X, that exists elsewhere. In this sense, the unconscious manifests itself in the symbolic order and emerges through the subject's encounter with a trans-individual symbolic order. There can be no unconscious without an-Other. The unconscious depends upon the existence of an-Other – an interlocutor, reader or analyst who can decipher its inscriptions. Similarly the subject of the unconscious, the subject of desire, is not the same as an individual human being, but something that is constituted in the gap between the signifier and the signified. The subject is the subject of the signifier insofar as it is marked by language. At the same time, the subject is the *breach* in the signifying chain – the gap that opens up between the symbolic and the real, through which the drive manifests itself. We will discuss these ideas further in the next chapter.

5

THE REAL

The real is one of Lacan's most difficult and at the same time most
interesting concepts. The difficulty of understanding the real is partly
due to the fact that it is not a 'thing'; it is not a material object in the
world or the human body or even 'reality'. For Lacan, our reality
consists of symbols and the process of signification. Therefore, what we
call reality is associated with the symbolic order or 'social reality'. The
real is the unknown that exists at the limit of this socio-symbolic
universe and is in constant tension with it. The real is also a very
paradoxical concept; it supports our social reality – the social world
cannot exist without it – but it also undermines that reality. A further
difficulty with understanding the real is that Lacan's conception of it
changed radically throughout his career. We will follow the development of the real from the 1950s, when it remained a relatively
underdeveloped concept, through the crucial period from 1964 to the
early 1970s, when Lacan used the concept to reformulate his understanding of the relationship between the imaginary and the symbolic,
to his late work, where the real is elevated to the central category
of his thought. Through each phase of his teaching Lacan placed a
different emphasis upon the real, although he also carried over the
preceding definitions and functions. Hence, like many of Lacan's
concepts, a consideration of the real forces us to reappraise and reformulate our previous understanding of his work. The real in late Lacan is

inseparable from an understanding of the role of fantasy, the *objet petit a* and *jouissance*. We will look at each of these important concepts in turn before illustrating the function of the real through Roland Barthes' exquisite final book *Camera Lucida*.

THE REAL IS ALWAYS IN ITS PLACE

From the 1950s until the early 1960s Lacan's creative energy was focused on elaborating the role of the signifier and the symbolic order. In this period the real performed an important function within his system, but it was relatively underdeveloped. Lacan used the term, *the* real, in his first published papers in the 1930s, but in these early texts it was essentially a philosophical concept designating 'absolute being' or 'being-in-itself'. Thus the real was conceptualized in opposition to the imaginary of the mirror phase. As 'being-in-itself', the real was beyond the realm of appearance and images.

In the Poe seminar of 1954–5, however, the concept underwent a significant revision and it was elevated to one of the three orders. As 'that which remains in its place', the real was opposed to both the imaginary and the symbolic. The relatively low status that Lacan accorded to the real at this time can be gauged from his account of it here as something that, like spat-out chewing gum in the street, remains glued to one's heel (Lacan 1988c [1956]: 40). During this early phase of his teaching, the real is described as 'concrete' – it is an indivisible brute materiality that exists prior to symbolization. From a clinical perspective, the real is the brute pre-symbolic reality that always returns to its place in the form of a need, such as hunger. The real is thus closely associated with the body prior to its symbolization, but it is important to keep in mind here that the real is the *need* that drives hunger not the *object* that satisfies it. When an infant feels hunger, this hunger can be temporarily satisfied through breast or bottle-feeding, but the breast and the bottle are the *objects* of hunger and in Lacanian psychoanalysis these objects are imaginary, as they can never fully satisfy the infant's demand. The real is the *place* from which that need originates and is pre-symbolic in the sense that we do not have any way of symbolizing it. We know that the real exists because we experience it and it enters discourse as a sign – the infant's crying, but the place from which it originates is beyond symbolization. The real, therefore, is not an object, a thing, but something that is repressed and functions unconsciously, intruding into our symbolic reality in the form of need. The real is a kind of ubiquitous undifferentiated mass from which we must distinguish ourselves, as subjects, through the process of symbolization. It is through the process of cancelling out, of symbolizing the real, that 'social reality' is created. In short, *the real does not exist*, as existence is a product of thought and language and the real precedes language. The real is 'that which resists symbolization absolutely'.

THE REAL AS THE LIMIT OF SYMBOLIZATION

From 1964 onwards the real is transformed in Lacan's thinking and loses any connection with biology or need. The concept continues to retain its association with brute matter, but its predominant meaning in Lacan at this time is as that which is unsymbolizable. The real is that which is beyond the symbolic and the imaginary and acts as a limit to both. Above all the real is associated with the concept of *trauma*.

In medicine a trauma is any kind of cut or wound, but we are probably much more familiar today with the idea of psychological trauma. For example, we hear and read a great deal in the media about *traumatic* events such as train crashes, wars or other human disasters. The effect of these events on the people present or just watching them is said to be traumatic and psychologically disturbing. To overcome these traumas sufferers usually require some form of counselling or therapy. The most common form of psychological trauma today is seen to be physical or sexual abuse, such as incest. For psychoanalysis, however, a trauma is not necessarily something that happens to a person 'in reality'. Instead, it is usually a *psychical* event. Psychic trauma arises from the confrontation between an external stimulus and the subject's inability to understand and master these excitations. Most commonly such confrontations arise from a subject's premature encounter with sexuality and the inability to comprehend what is taking place. This event then leaves a psychological scar in the subject's unconscious that will resurface in later life. For Freud, the notion of trauma is linked to the primal scene, whereby a child has either a real or imaginary experience that it cannot comprehend. This inassimilable memory is forgotten and repressed until some later, perhaps insignificant, event brings it back to consciousness.

The idea of trauma implies that there is a certain blockage or fixation in the process of signification. Trauma arrests the movement of symbolization and fixes the subject in an earlier phase of development. A memory, for example, is fixed in a person's mind causing them intense mental disturbance and suffering and no matter how they try to rationalize and express this memory, it keeps returning and repeating the suffering. What Lacan adds to the Freudian conception of trauma is the notion that trauma is *real* insofar as it remains unsymbolizable and is a permanent dislocation at the very heart of the subject. The experience of trauma also reveals how the real can never be completely absorbed into the symbolic, into social reality. No matter how often we try to put our pain and suffering into language, to symbolize it, there is always something left over. In other words, there is always a residue that cannot be transformed through language. This excess, this 'X' as Lacan will call it, is the real. As we will see, the real thus becomes associated with the death drive and *jouissance*, as Lacan increasingly emphasizes the *impossibility* of the encounter with the real. But first let us say something about how an object can *not* exist but at the same time profoundly affect our lives.

DAS DING (THE THING)

During the second phase of Lacan's teaching the real loses the sense of 'thingness' which his earlier conception had retained. In his seminar on the ethics of psychoanalysis (1959–60) Lacan sought to clarify Freud's definition of the unconscious and especially the question of what is repressed. For Freud there can be no unconscious without repression, but what exactly is it that is repressed: words, images, feelings? This question has led to many disputes and is one reason why there are so many different schools of psychoanalysis. For Lacan, what is repressed is not images, words or emotions but something much more fundamental. Freud hit upon this when, in *The Interpretation of Dreams*, he suggested that there was a hard impenetrable core of the dream – what he called the 'navel' of the dream – that is beyond interpretation. What is repressed, argues Lacan, is this hard impenetrable core. There is always a core of the real that is missing from the symbolic and all other representations, images and signifiers are no more than attempts to fill this gap. In seminar VII Lacan identified this repressed element as *the representative of the representation*, or *das Ding* (the Thing).

The Thing is the beyond of the signified – that which is unknowable in itself. It is something beyond symbolization, and therefore associated with the real, or as Lacan puts it, 'the thing in its dumb reality' (1992 [1986]: 55). The Thing is a lost object that must be continually re-found. However, it is more importantly an 'object that is nowhere articulated, it is a lost object, but paradoxically an object that was never there in the first place to be lost' (1992 [1986]: 58). The Thing is 'the cause of the most fundamental human passion' (1992 [1986]: 97); it is the object-cause of desire and can only be constituted retrospectively. The Thing is 'objectively' speaking *no-thing*; it is only something in relation to the desire that constitutes it. After the seminar of 1959–60 the concept of *das Ding* completely disappeared from Lacan's work and it was replaced in 1964 by the idea of the *objet petit a*. What is important to keep in mind here with respect to the real is that the Thing is *no-thing* and only becomes something through the desire of the subject. It is the desire to fill the emptiness or void at the core of subjectivity and the symbolic that creates the Thing, as opposed to the loss of some original Thing creating the desire to find it. In Chapter 4 we saw how Lacan designated this process as *separation*. In his later work Lacan supplemented the idea of separation with the notion of fantasy and what he described as *traversing the fundamental fantasy*.

UNCONSCIOUS FANTASY

Psychoanalysis is primarily concerned with the reality of our unconscious desires and wishes and not with social reality. These unconscious desires are manifested through fantasy. Fantasy is an imagined scene in which the subject is a protagonist, and always represents the fulfilment of a wish (in the last analysis, an unconscious wish) in a manner that is distorted to a greater or lesser extent by defensive processes. Fantasy is intrinsic to sexuality and is one of the central concerns of psychoanalysis. As we will see later, fantasies are never a purely private affair but circulate in the public domain through such media as film, literature and television. Fantasies, therefore, are at once universal and particular. There are a limited number of themes or primary narratives that consistently reappear in fantasy scenarios, but these can be endlessly reworked through the contingent material of a subject's everyday life.

Fantasies are generally a combination of both conscious and unconscious elements, existing between the poles of reality and imagination. There are essentially three kinds of reality for Freud:

1   material or physical reality
2   the psychological, or the reality of our intermediate thoughts
3   psychical reality, or the reality of unconscious wishes, that is, fantasy.

(Laplanche and Pontalis 1986 [1968]: 8)

Freud's conception of psychical reality often means little more than the reality of our thoughts and personal world, but nonetheless it is as real as material reality. Fantasy exists in this realm of *psychical reality*. Laplanche and Pontalis distinguish two types of fantasy: *original* or *primal* fantasies and *secondary* fantasies. Secondary fantasy concerns daydreams and the reworking of ready-made scenarios, and are not my direct concern here. The original or primal fantasy on the other hand is a more complex affair. Original, primal, fantasies are universal and limited in number; the Oedipus complex, for example, functions in this way as a universal fantasy structure. Primal fantasies are not original in the sense that they are the origin of all subsequent fantasies, but rather they are *fantasies of origins* – the scene of fantastical origins that Freud elaborated in *Totem and Taboo* for instance. Primal fantasies set the pattern for a subject's later psychic life and in this sense are 'structuring' rather than representing a fixed content. We will see how this structuring takes place in relation to sexual difference in Chapter 6.

Fantasy originates in 'auto-eroticism' and the hallucinatory satisfaction of the drive. 'In the absence of a real object', write Laplanche and Pontalis, 'the infant reproduces the experience of the original satisfaction in a hallucinated form' (1986 [1968]: 24). Thus, our most fundamental fantasies are linked to our very earliest experiences of the rise and resolution of desire. The important point here is the nature of the relationship between fantasy and desire; 'fantasy *is not the object of desire, but its setting*' (1986 [1968]: 26, my italics). Fantasy is the way in which subjects structure or organize their desire; it is the support of desire. In the previous chapter we saw how the subject is faced with the enigma of the desire of the Other and is forced to pose certain questions to itself, such as: 'What am I in the Other's desire?' Fantasy is a response to that question. It is through fantasy that we learn how to desire and we are constituted as desiring subjects. The space of fantasy, writes Žižek, 'functions as an empty surface, as a kind of screen for the projection of desires' (1992: 8). We can clearly see here one reason why Lacanianism might be attractive to film studies. Fantasy is not the object of desire, neither is it the desire for specific objects; it is the setting or the *mise-en-scène* of desire. The pleasure we derive from fantasy does not result from the achievement of its aim, its object, but rather from the staging of desire in the first place. The whole point of fantasy is that it should never be fulfilled or confused with reality. The crucial term that mediates between fantasy and the real is the *objet petit a*.

FANTASY AND THE *OBJET PETIT A*

Lacan consistently reformulated the *objet petit a* from his earliest work to his final seminars in the 1970s. The *objet a* is implicated in all three of Lacan's orders. The algebraic sign *a* was first introduced by Lacan in 1955 in relation to the schema L, where it designates the little other, *autre*, as opposed to the capitalized A of the big Other. The *objet a* represents the Other's lack not in the sense of a specific object that is lacking but as lack itself. What does Lacan mean by this? Desire, strictly speaking, has no object. Desire is always the desire for something that is missing and thus involves a constant search for the missing object. Through the rupture between subject and Other a gap is opened up between the desire of the child and that of the mother. It is this gap that inaugurates the movement of desire and the advent of the *objet petit a*. Through fantasy, the subject attempts to sustain the illusion of unity with the Other and ignore his or her own division. Although the desire of the Other always exceeds or escapes the subject, there nevertheless remains something that the subject can recover and thus sustains him or herself. This something is the *objet a*.

The *objet a* is not, therefore, an object we have lost, because then we would be able to find it and satisfy our desire. It is rather the constant sense we have, as subjects, that something is lacking or missing from our lives. We are always searching for fulfilment, for knowledge, for possessions, for love, and whenever we achieve these goals there is always something more we desire; we cannot quite pinpoint it but we know that it is there. This is one sense in which we can understand the Lacanian real as the void or abyss at the core of our being that we constantly try to fill out. The *objet a* is both the void, the gap, and whatever object momentarily comes to fill that gap in our symbolic reality. What is important to keep in mind here is that the *objet a* is not the object itself but the function of masking the lack. As Parveen Adams writes:

> [T]he object is not part of the signifying chain; it is a 'hole' in that chain. It is a hole in the field of representation, but it does not simply ruin representation. It mends it as it ruins it. It both produces a hole and is what comes to the place of lack to cover it over.

> (1996a: 151)

Like so many of Lacan's concepts, the paradox of desire is that it functions retrospectively. As with *das Ding*, the *objet a* is, 'objectively' speaking, nothing. It only exists as something in relation to the desire that brings it about. If you think about falling in love this will help you to understand what Lacan means. When you first fall in love you idealize the other person and feel perfect together. This is the imaginary dimension of being in love. There is also the symbolic dimension of being 'a couple' and of being in a relationship with another subject who is lacking. But there is also something more; your new partner may be beautiful, intelligent, funny, a great dancer but then so is everyone else. So what is it that makes your new partner special? There is something elusive, something intangible, something extra about them and you cannot quite grasp or articulate it but you know it is there. That is why you love them. This is the *objet a* – the object-cause of your desire. The *objet a* then is at once the void, the gap, the lack around which the symbolic order is structured and that which comes to mask or cover over that lack. The '*Object (a) is the leftover of that process of constituting an object; the scrap that evades the grasp of symbolization*' (Fink 1995: 94). The *objet a*, in other words, is the left-over of the real; it is that which escapes symbolization and is beyond representation. In Lacanian terms, fantasy defines a subject's 'impossible' relation to the *objet a*.

THE IMPOSSIBILITY OF THE REAL AND *JOUISSANCE*

It is this sense of the real as an impossible encounter that will dominate the final phase of Lacan's teaching in the 1970s. Indeed, he increasingly comes to see the whole experience of psychoanalysis as circling around this impossible traumatic encounter. In this phase the key distinction Lacan makes is not between ego and subject, imaginary and symbolic, or even between alienation and separation, but between the real and reality. Lacan's elaboration of fantasy as the support for reality serves to operate as a defence against the intrusion of the real into our everyday experience. Lacan called this process 'traversing the fantasy'. Traversing the fantasy involves the subject subjectifying the trauma of the real. In other words, the subject takes the traumatic event upon him/herself and assumes responsibility for that *jouissance*. *Jouissance* is a very complicated notion in Lacan and not directly translatable into English. The term is usually translated as 'enjoyment' but, as we will see, it involves a combination of pleasure and pain, or, more accurately, pleasure *in* pain. *Jouissance* expresses that paradoxical situation where patients appear to enjoy their own illness or symptom. In French the word also has sexual connotations and is associated with sexual pleasure. The example of *jouissance* that Lacan usually provides, however, is of religious or mystical ecstatic experience.

Although Lacan used the term *jouissance* as early as 1953, it only became a prominent concept in his work in the 1960s, when it was associated with the drive and the real. In *Beyond the Pleasure Principle* (1984b [1920]) Freud was forced to revise his earlier theory of the drives that asserted the primacy of pleasure principle, that is to say, the theory that our primary motivation as human beings is the fulfilment of pleasure or desire. Clinical experience revealed to Freud that subjects compulsively repeated painful or traumatic experiences in direct contradiction to the primacy of the pleasure principle. Freud called this beyond of pleasure 'the death drive' and suggested that the primary purpose of life is to find the correct path to death. Lacan followed Freud in associating the death drive with repetition, but he argued that we are not driven *towards* death but *by* death. It is loss that drives life through desire but, as Ellie Ragland-Sullivan puts it, human beings will settle for any experience, however painful, rather than fall out of the familiarity of the symbolic into the trauma and void of the real (1995: 94). Ragland-Sullivan describes *jouissance* as 'the essence or quality that gives one's life its value' (1995: 88). Contrary to desire which moves from one signifier to another constantly trying to satisfy itself, *jouissance* is absolute and certain (remember that the primary and defining characteristic of all drives is the consistency of pressure). Thus, Lacan opposed *jouissance* to desire and suggested that desire seeks satisfaction in the consistency of *jouissance*. Whether we like it or not the symbolic is governed by the death drive. Death is the beyond of pleasure, the inaccessible, the forbidden – the ultimate limit that cannot be overcome; and this ultimate limit is also related to *jouissance*.

The difficulty with talking about *jouissance* is that we cannot actually say what it is. We experience it rather through its absence or insufficiency. As subjects we are driven by insatiable desires. As we seek to realize our desires we will inevitably be disappointed – the satisfaction we achieve is never quite enough; we always have the sense that there is something more, something we have missed out on, something more we could have had. This something more that would satisfy and fulfil us beyond the meagre pleasure we experience is *jouissance*. We do not know what it is but assume that it must be there because we are constantly dissatisfied. As Fink puts it, eventually 'we think that there must be something better, we say that there must be something better, we *believe* that there must be something better' (2002: 35) to such an extent that we give it consistency; we retrospectively turn nothing into something. Furthermore, in assuming that it is there and that we are lacking it we generally attribute it to the Other. The Other is believed to experience a level of enjoyment beyond our own experience. The important point here is that this unfailing *jouissance* does not exist:

> [I]t *insists* as an ideal, an idea, a possibility thought permits us to envision. In [Lacan's] terminology, it 'ex-sists': it persists and makes its claims felt with a certain insistence from the outside, as it were. Outside in the sense that it is not a wish [desire], 'Let's do *that* again!' but, rather, 'Isn't there something else you could do, something different you could try?'
>
> (Fink 2002: 35)

This belief in the excessive *jouissance* of the Other is sustained through fantasy. Fantasy is one of the ways through which we reconcile ourselves to our dissatisfaction with our own *jouissance* and the impossibility of the real. Through fantasy we construct our social reality as an answer to the intractability of the real. This is also, as you will have realized, the structure of racism and anti-Semitism that I outlined previously; what we assume the Other – be they Jewish, black, gypsies or gay – has stolen from us is our *jouissance*. In the following chapter we will look at the question of *jouissance* in more detail and the distinction Lacan makes between 'masculine' and 'feminine' *jouissance*, but first let me provide an application of the concepts of the real and *objet a* from the field of cultural studies.

ROLAND BARTHES' *CAMERA LUCIDA*

Camera Lucida is a beautiful and poignant study of death and loss, made all the more so by the accident of its place within Barthes' oeuvre. Written after the death of his mother and shortly before his own death, it was Barthes' final book and therefore has a sense of finality about it, as Barthes' last word. The sense of Barthes having his final say is reinforced by the style of the text. *Camera Lucida* presents itself as very much a subjective meditation on the *essence* of photography. It is a quest, an inner journey, an 'ontological' desire, as Barthes puts it, to discover 'what photography was "in itself," by what essential feature it was distinguished from the community of images' (1984 [1980]: 3). *Camera Lucida* then appears to abandon Barthes' earlier semiotic attempt to elaborate a grammar of the text in 'Introduction to the Structural Analysis of Narrative' (1977a [1966]), as well as his more fragmentary, playful and delirious style associated with *The Pleasure of Text* (1990 [1973]). With its dedication to Sartre and its phenomenological emphasis on the 'thing-in-itself' it would appear to mark a return to origins; a return to Barthes' own phenomenological roots and a more humanistic approach to texts. We should not be too hasty, however, in reaching for such explanations. *Camera Lucida* commences: 'One day, quite some time ago, I happened on a photograph of Napoleon's youngest brother, . . .' (1984 [1980]: 3). It thus announces itself at the outset as not so much a work of theory but a work of fiction. The 'I' in this text is as much a textual construction as the 'I' in any other fictional text and it should not be confused with the 'real' Roland Barthes. If *Camera Lucida* has the sense of being Barthes' last word, we should recall that Barthes' whole life's work was dedicated to the idea that there can be no final word. Once a text is in the public domain, as Barthes taught us in 'The Death of the Author' (1977b [1968]), the author is no longer the arbiter of its meaning. We should be alert therefore to the fact that there is something else going on in this text and we might consider it not so much a theory of the essence of photography as an 'autobiographical novel' (Burgin 1986: 88).

THE *STUDIUM* AND THE *PUNCTUM*

What attracts Barthes to photography is the relationship between particular photographs and their referent; the photograph, he writes, 'is literally an emanation of the referent' (1984 [1980]: 80). Whereas language by its very nature is fictional, the photograph has a sense of certainty and authenticity. For Barthes, then, a specific photograph can never be distinguished from its referent. It carries it with itself, or, to put it another way, the referent appears to adhere to the photograph (or stick to its heel, as Lacan would say). This, argues Barthes, is the essence of photography. There are two necessary elements to any photograph, which he calls the *studium* and the *punctum*. The *studium* is the general field of cultural interest aroused by the photograph. It is the shared or common ground of cultural meaning – the *average* effect that the photograph produces in spectators, whether one likes or dislikes a particular photograph. The *punctum* on the other hand is a more private and personal experience; it is that which punctuates the *studium* and arouses our specific interest in the photograph. The *punctum* is that contingent, accidental element in the photograph that captures our attention. As Barthes says, it is that which pricks me, but also bruises me and is poignant for me. If the *studium* refers to the general overall sense of the photograph, then the *punctum* is the detail that disrupts its smooth surface. It is the detail that attracts one to the photograph and which Barthes compares with a 'partial' object. The *punctum* has a certain expansive, metonymic power, as it leads one from one association to the next. As such the *punctum* also works retrospectively. It is not something that can be staged or placed in the photograph, but rather is the detail we recall once we are no longer in front of the photograph and we think back upon it.

MOURNING THE REAL

Camera Lucida is quite explicitly a work of mourning, but the specific occasion for these reflections was the discovery of an old photograph:

> I was [Barthes writes] looking for the truth of the face I loved. And I found it. The photograph was very old. The corners were blunted from having been pasted into an album, the sepia print had faded, and the picture just managed to show two children standing together at the end of a little wooden bench in

a glassed-in conservatory, what was called a Winter Garden in those days. My mother was five at the time (1898), her brother seven.

(1984 [1980]: 67)

This photograph brings forth a series of reflections on photography, psychoanalysis, life and death, but we never actually see the photograph itself. *Camera Lucida*, in other words, is structured around an absent centre (Iversen 1994). The text continually circles around this absence and produces a series of substitute photographs that fill the hole left by the original loss, but we can never get back to that original experience itself. The text never produces, indeed it can never produce, the Truth, the thing-in-itself, the essence that Barthes is searching for. The absent photograph of his mother functions as a lost object in the psychoanalytic sense that it was never there in the first place. Barthes can never recover the truth of the face that he loved because all that remains of it are the representations as left-overs of that impossible encounter.

So where does this leave Barthes' argument that the relationship to the referent is the essence of photography? The photographic referent is not the referent of other sign systems; it is not an '*optionally* real thing to which an image or a sign refers but the *necessarily* real thing which has been placed before the lens, without which there would be no photograph' (1984 [1980]: 76). Unlike painting or language, photography can never deny its past, that the thing existed and was there in front of the camera, but that real is lost the moment the photograph itself comes into being. And it is this that is the very essence of photography – its *noeme*, that is to say, its 'that-has-been' or its intractability. Another name for this is 'the real' in the full Lacanian sense. Psychoanalysis, Lacan tells us in seminar XI, is essentially an encounter with the real that eludes us (1979 [1973]: 53) and the term he uses to describe this encounter is *tuché*. Barthes' text is haunted by this encounter – the encounter with the 'that-has-been' essence of photography, the intractability of the real and of grasping one's own mortality. The *tuché* presents itself in the form of trauma, that is to say, that which is impossible for the subject to bear and to assimilate. It is this notion of trauma as the hard impenetrable kernel at the heart of subjectivity that structures Barthes' text and his conception of photographic essence. As Victor Burgin has pointed out, 'trauma' derives from the Greek word for 'wound'; its Latin equivalent is 'punctum' (1986: 86).

In other words, Barthes' detail that pricks us, bruises us and disrupts the *studium* (the symbolic) of the photograph is that fleeting glimpse, or encounter with the real as *objet petit a*.

SUMMARY

Lacan's concept of 'the real' is among his most fascinating concepts. The category of the real developed from an early marginal status to being the central category of Lacan's later work. The real is that which resists symbolization; it is the traumatic kernel at the core of subjectivity and the symbolic order. The real is thus associated with the death drive and *jouissance* as the ultimate, unspeakable, limit of human existence. *Jouissance* is opposed to desire – it is the dissatisfaction that we experience with the failure of our desire – and it is through fantasy and the *objet petit a* that the subject sustains themselves in this impossible scenario. With these concepts Lacan revolutionized the practice of psychoanalysis and its implication for other disciplines. We will now turn to one of Lacan's last seminars and one of the most contentious areas of his theory: Lacan's account of sexual difference.

6

SEXUAL DIFFERENCE

Let us finally consider what is surely the most controversial and contested area of Lacanian psychoanalysis: the conceptualization of feminine sexuality. Lacan's provocative slogans, such as 'the woman does not exist' and 'there is no such thing as a sexual relationship', have been greeted with indignation and outrage as well as prolonged and passionate defence. Lacan's thinking on feminine sexuality is distinguished by two main phases: first, he was concerned to distinguish sexual difference on the basis of the phallus and here Lacan makes a significant innovation regarding Freudian thinking. For Freud the question of sexual difference revolved around the 'castration complex', that is, around whether or not someone 'has' or 'does not have' a penis. For Lacan, on the other hand, castration is a symbolic process that involves the cutting off, not of one's penis, but of one's *jouissance* and the recognition of lack. In order to represent this lack the subject has two possible alternatives – that of 'having' or 'being' the phallus (Adams 1966b). According to Lacan, masculinity involves the posture or pretence of having the phallus, while femininity involves the *masquerade* of being the phallus. The second phase of Lacan's thinking on sexual difference comes from a late seminar, seminar XX – *Encore: On Feminine Sexuality, The Limits of Love and Knowledge 1972–1973* – and concerns the 'structures of sexuation'. In this late phase Lacan continues to develop masculinity and femininity as structures that are available to both men and women and not related to one's biology, but what now determines a masculine and feminine structure is the type of *jouissance* one is able to attain – what Lacan called phallic *jouissance* and Other *jouissance*. We will explore these highly controversial ideas below before presenting an example of what Lacan means by them in the form of the poetic tradition of courtly love.

FREUD AND THE ENIGMA OF FEMININE SEXUALITY

Freud based his theory of the Oedipus complex and infantile sexuality on the experience of boys, and at first he thought that the same process could simply be transferred to girls but in reverse. Gradually Freud was forced to acknowledge, by the weight of his own clinical experience and the research of his colleagues, that this was an untenable position. Two factors came into play here. First, the realization that, in the final phase of the Oedipus complex, its dissolution, it is not the genitals themselves that are in question but the presence or absence of the male genital organ, the penis. Second, a number of Freud's followers began to look much more closely at the pre-Oedipal phase of an infant's life and in particular at the importance of the mother/child relationship. Freud came to accept the importance of this early pre-Oedipal phase of development, but this meant that he had to revise his early conception of the Oedipus complex. In the pre-Oedipal phase both sexes are equally attached to the mother as the first love object and what Freud needed to explain was how girls shift from their mother to their father as a love object for the Oedipus complex to even start.

The Oedipus complex remains fairly straightforward for boys; they initially see their mother as a love object but slowly realize that their mother is also the love object of their father. The father thus becomes a rival for the mother and the boy fears that the father will cut off his penis. The boy resolves this dilemma by giving up the mother as a love object and identifying with the father. As compensation for giving up on the mother the boy will be able to have other women as love objects in the future. For girls, however, the Oedipus complex has to account for the process whereby girls first give up their initial love-object (the mother). The Oedipus complex for girls, thus, involves an extra, earlier, step. The girl transfers her love from the mother to the father, because she realizes that neither she nor her mother has a penis, in a process that Freud called penis envy. The mother is then transformed from an object of love to a rival for the father's affections. At first the girl devalues the mother because she does not possess a penis and then resents her for making her the same. The problem for Freud was that he simply could not then explain why a girl should give up the father as love object and re-identify with the mother.

The castration complex marks the conclusion and resolution of the Oedipus complex for boys, that is to say, boys give up on the other as love object. For girls, on the other hand, it is the castration complex that leads up to the Oedipus complex and there is no satisfactory resolution of it. The girl must accept that she does not have the penis in order to transfer her desire to her father, but in doing so she does not accept this loss without some kind of compensation. Freud speculated that this compensation takes the form of desiring a baby from the father and the female Oedipus complex culminates, not in the threat of castration, but in the desire for the gift of a baby from the father. Thus girls never fully resolve their Oedipus complex because they can never completely give up on the other as love object. As we can see, the Oedipus complex for girls is a much more complex affair than for boys and it is also deeply unsatisfactory as a concept.

Freud's speculations on the female Oedipus complex led him to explore the nature of feminine sexuality but resulted only in a series of unanswered questions. Until the end of his life Freud was bewildered by the enigma of feminine sexuality. He described femininity as a 'dark continent' and never resolved the question 'what does woman want?' In the 1920s the failure of psychoanalysis to adequately account for the development of female sexuality gave rise to what has been called the first great debate on feminine sexuality. This debate was initiated through a paper by one of Freud's closest associates, Ernest Jones (1879–1958), which drew responses from many of the most prominent women psychoanalysts of the time, including Karen Horney (1885–1952), Melanie Klein (1882–1960) and Joan Riviere (1883–1962) (see Juliet Mitchell's introduction to *Feminine Sexuality* (Mitchell and Rose 1982) for an account of this debate). Lacan's work on feminine sexuality is a continuation of these debates from the 1920s and 1930s and subsequently gave rise to the 'second great debate' in the 1970s and 1980s (see Brennan 1989).

TO HAVE OR TO BE THE PHALLUS?

The feminist critique of psychoanalysis focused on two particularly problematic strands of Freud's thought. First, feminists saw psycho-analysis as propagating a form of biological essentialism in the sense that one's anatomy – whether or not one has or does not have a penis – determines one's sexual identity. And there is indeed more than a little truth in this. Marie Bonaparte (1882–1962), for example, went so far as to argue that 'biology is destiny' and the attempts to revise Freud's 'phallocentrism' by Jones, Bonaparte and Horney had paradoxically resulted in much more deterministic and essentialist theories of sexual development. The second critique advanced by feminism is that psychoanalysis always defines women negatively in relation to men. For Freud, men are seen as active agents while women are defined in terms of passivity. By the 1960s and early 1970s these two critiques were firmly established and widely accepted within feminism (see Kate Millet's classic feminist text *Sexual Politics* (1977 [1969]) for a clear statement of these criticisms), and consequently the psychoanalytic explanation of sexual difference was displaced through the study of gender as a social construct. It was within this context that Lacan's idio-syncratic formulations of sexual difference were received. Lacan's insistence that all notions of a stable fixed identity are a fiction rather than biologically given were seen to provide feminists with the possi-bility of a non-essentialist psychoanalytic theory of sexual difference.

From a Lacanian perspective the unconscious is that which under-mines any stable or fixed identity and that includes a stable sexual identity. For early Lacan, sexual difference is not a question of biology but of signification; masculinity and femininity are not anatomically given but are subject positions defined through their relationship to the phallus as signifier. As we saw previously, for Lacan, the phallus is a signifier that is related, but not directly equivalent, to the penis and, as Jacqueline Rose points out, the importance of the phallus as signifier is precisely 'that its status in the development of human sexu-ality is something which nature *cannot* account for' (1996a: 63). The phallus is the signifier of lack. The phallus functions initially as an imaginary object – an object presumed to satisfy the mother's desire. It then functions symbolically through the recognition that desire cannot be satisfied and that as an object it will remain beyond reach. The rupturing of the imaginary unity between mother and child inaugurates the movement of desire and simultaneously the process of signification. The phallus thus represents a moment of rupture or division that re-enacts the fundamental division of the subject. In this sense, the phallus represents lack for both boys and girls, as both sexes are symbolically castrated. Castration for Lacan is a very different process from that elaborated by Freud and involves a fundamental loss for both sexes, that is to say, the giving up of some part of one's *jouissance*. In order to come into being as desiring subjects we are forced to acknowledge the impossibility of the total fulfilment of our *jouissance*. Castration designates that fundamental loss for which the phallus is the signifier. What we need to keep in mind here, if we are not to confuse these terms and, more importantly, if we are not to confuse them with the actual physical organ, is that *jouissance* is related to the drive and the real, while the phallus is a signifier and is related to the symbolic. The 'difference' between a male and a female castration complex, therefore, is how the subject represents this primordial lack or loss, and it is here that the asymmetry of the Oedipus complex becomes apparent. Boys can 'pretend' to *have* the phallus, while girls must *be* the phallus. What does this mean? Having and being the phallus represents two modes of identification that cover over this primary lack. Through the Oedipus complex boys recognize the mother's desire and lack. They then identify her object of desire with the father, assuming that he has the phallus. In short, the boy shifts from the mother as a lacking other to the father as possessor of the phallus. Thus, boys *pretend* to have the object of desire for the Other (women). This is only 'pretence', however, because they never possessed the phallus in the first place; the phallus is always elsewhere.

Women, on the other hand, have to undergo the rather more complex procedure of giving up on the notion of 'having' the phallus before they can identify with the mother and thus become the object of desire for the Other (men). Lacan linked this process through which women must give up an essential part of themselves in order to *be* the phallus with the concept of masquerade:

> Paradoxical as this formulation may seem, I am saying that it is in order to be the phallus, that is to say, the signifier of the desire of the Other, that a woman will reject an essential part of femininity, namely, all her attributes in the masquerade. It is for that which she is not that she wishes to be desired as well as loved.
>
> (Lacan 1977d [1958]: 289–90)

It is through the masquerade that a woman's 'not-having' the phallus is transformed into 'being' the phallus.

FEMININITY AS MASQUERADE

Lacan developed the notion of masquerade from Joan Riviere's paper, 'Womanliness as Masquerade' (1986 [1929]). This was a response to an earlier paper by Ernest Jones entitled 'Early Development of Female Sexuality' (1927). Jones had distinguished between two types of female sexual development: so-called 'normal' heterosexual development and homosexual development, that is, women who sought male recognition for their masculinity. Riviere was concerned to introduce a new type of woman into psychoanalytic considerations of femininity – a particular character type that was much more resonant with contemporary woman than anything Freud or Jones had previously considered, that is, the 'intellectual woman'. For Riviere, this new type of woman raises the difficult issue of how to address the anxiety that they raise in men. Women who aspire to 'masculine' or intellectual pursuits arouse fear and anxiety in the very men they wish to be colleagues and collaborators with. Therefore, 'women who wish for masculinity may put on a mask of womanliness to avert anxiety and the retribution feared from men' (Riviere 1986 [1929]: 35). Riviere's suggestion that womanliness is worn as a mask appears to have much wider significance, however, than just in the case of intellectual women. She writes that womanliness 'could be assumed and worn as a mask, both to hide the possession of masculinity and to avert the reprisals expected if she was found to possess it' (1986 [1929]: 38), but if we are to ask what distinguishes genuine womanliness and womanliness as masquerade they appear to be the same thing. What is radical in Riviere's position, write Appignanesi and Forrester, 'is that for her mask and essence are one where womanliness is concerned' (1993: 363).

Riviere saw the notion of masquerade as an important contribution to the theory of female sexual development, identifying it at work in the female Oedipus complex. She argues that both the mother and the father are the little girl's rivals and objects of her sadistic fury:

> In this appalling predicament the girl's only safety lies in placating the
> mother and atoning for her crime [destroying the woman's body]. She must

> retire from rivalry with the mother and, if she can, endeavour to restore to her what she has stolen. As we know, she identifies herself with her father; and then uses the masculinity she thus obtains by putting it at the service of the mother. She becomes the father and takes his place; so she can 'restore' him to the mother.

(1986 [1929]: 41)

The father, however, must be placated and appeased too and this can only be achieved by masquerading in a feminine guise for him, that is showing him her 'love' and guiltlessness towards him. According to Riviere, the little girl is caught in a double bind between appeasing her mother and appeasing her father, but this is by no means a symmetrical relationship: 'the task of guarding herself against the woman's retribution is harder than with the man; her efforts to placate and make reparation by restoring and using the penis in the mother's service were never enough' (1986 [1929]: 42). In terms of women's identity and sexual development, then, she must first identify with the father and only then with the mother. The problem for women, therefore, is not whether they put on the mask of femininity or not but *how well it fits*. In short, *femininity is masquerade*.

Riviere's notion of masquerade raises important and difficult questions in relation to feminine sexuality. The assumption of the mask implies that there is something hidden behind it. In other words, behind the artifice of the masquerade lies the genuine, authentic, woman. For Riviere, however, the appearance and the essence of feminine sexuality are one and the same. It is this dilemma, the conflation of genuine womanliness and masquerade, that Lacan elaborates. Lacan sees in the notion of masquerade 'the feminine sexual attitude' par excellence, that is to say, it is the mask or veil that 'is constitutive of the feminine libidinal structure' (Heath 1986: 52). In other words, 'masquerade is a representation of femininity but then femininity is representation, the representation of the woman' (Heath 1986: 53). What the notion of masquerade foregrounds is not the *essential* identity of women but rather the *constructed* nature of that identity: 'The masquerade says that the woman exists at the same time that, as masquerade, it says she does not' (Heath 1986: 54).

THE WOMAN DOES NOT EXIST

The idea that 'Woman does not exist' (Lacan 1998 [1975]: 7) or that she is 'not-whole' has often been seen as some the most offensive of Lacan's formulations about feminine sexuality but, as with the notion of the phallus, this reading is based on a fundamental misreading of Lacan. Just as the phallus is an 'empty' signifier – it is a signifier of lack and has no positive content – the sign 'woman' has no positive or empirical signified. There is no universal category of women to which the sign 'Woman' refers. To appeal to the notion of women therefore as a homogeneous group is to appeal to an imaginary, and therefore illusory, identity. Furthermore, when Lacan talks about existence, he is referring to something at the level of the symbolic. If the woman was to exist she would have to exist at the level of the symbolic and this has a number of implications. First, as the symbolic is phallic by definition, it would subordinate femininity to the phallus in the same way that Freud saw femininity as defined by not having the penis. Second, it would mean that femininity is wholly a discursive construct and that sexual identity is completely socially – symbolically – constructed. Lacan, however, 'leaves open the possibility of there being something – a feminine *jouissance* – that is unlocatable in experience, that cannot, then, be said to exist in the symbolic order' (Copjec 1994a: 224). To say that the woman is 'not-whole' is not to say that she is in some way incomplete and lacking something that the man has, but rather that she is 'defined as *not* wholly hemmed in. A woman is not split in the same way as a man; though alienated, she is not altogether subject to the symbolic order' (Fink 1995: 107). Lacan puts this in a rather convoluted double negative, which has given rise to much of the misunderstanding about woman as 'not-all':

> [A]nd this is the whole point, she has different ways of approaching that phallus and of keeping it for herself. It's not because she is not-wholly in the phallic function that she is not there at all. She is *not* not at all there. She is there in full. But there is something more.
>
> (1998 [1975]: 74)

It is precisely because the woman does not exist and that she is 'not-whole' that she has access to something more (encore) than men.

ENCORE: THE THEORY OF SEXUATION

In his early account of sexual difference Lacan had tried to free psychoanalysis from its essentialism and normative, heterosexual, bias by
transposing the Freudian understanding of castration and penis envy on
to the phallus as a signifier of lack. While the notion of masquerade has
been extraordinarily productive in terms of analysing the representation of women (see 'After Lacan'), it still left completely unanswered
the question of feminine desire. In 1972–3 Lacan returned to this issue
– what can be said about feminine desire – in the seminar *Encore*. In
this seminar Lacan further developed the idea that masculinity and
femininity are not biologically given, but designate two 'sexed' subject
positions that are available to both men and women. What is important
in this seminar is that masculinity and femininity are defined not simply
in relation to the phallus, but through the type of *jouissance* that is
attainable in each position. Sexual difference, therefore, is determined
not as a difference between two discrete sexes but as a result of one's
position in relation to *jouissance*.

Encore is usually read as Lacan's final statement on feminine sexuality, but this is only part of the picture. Seminar XX presents a
wide-ranging reflection on the nature of love, *jouissance* and the limits
of knowledge. Sexual difference is important here because, from a
psychoanalytic perspective, it is the ultimate limit of knowledge.
Sexual difference is reducible to neither nature nor culture, but
emerges at the point of their intersection. This does not mean that
sexual identity is the sum of natural (biological) and cultural (signifying) elements, but rather that it is that which is left out of their unity.
What Lacan is driving at here is that all structures, whether of the
subject or the symbolic, are necessarily incomplete; there is always
some contingent element that is left out, an exception to the rule.
Thus, seminar XX should be read as a continuation of the project Lacan
set out in seminar XI, when he began to elaborate the *objet petit a* as
the left-over of the real. *Encore* is also, as we will see, a continuation
of seminar VII and the discussion of courtly love that Lacan introduced
there. Increasingly, in the late Lacan, the drive is associated with the
exception and limit; it is the concept of the drive that means that the
subject is not wholly determined by the symbolic and marks the limit
of the signifier upon the subject. The drive is also the terrain upon
which sex is played out.

MASCULINITY

As we have seen throughout this introduction, the lesson of psycho-analysis, or what we can call the tragedy of psychoanalysis, is that the subject is inherently divided and can never be satisfied. Further-more, our knowledge is always limited by that unknown we call the unconscious. We are plagued as subjects by the anxiety that our *jouis-sance* – our pleasure or enjoyment – is never enough. In other words, we are driven by an inherent dissatisfaction and sense of insufficiency. We constantly have the sense that there is something *more*; we do not know what this is, but we have the sense that it is there, and we want it. This is what Fink refers to as a 'paltry' *jouissance* (2002: 36) and it is the form of *jouissance* that Lacan identifies as phallic jouissance. 'Phallic jouissance is the jouissance that fails us, that disappoints us. It is susceptible to failure, and fundamentally misses our partner' (Fink 2002: 37).

Phallic *jouissance* is that form of enjoyment that most of us experi-ence most of the time; that is to say, just when we think we possess our object of desire – be that another person, a new possession or even a difficult idea we have been struggling to get hold of – we are still dissatisfied; we are disappointed and have a sense that our desire has not been fully satisfied. This sense of (dis)satisfaction that always leaves something wanting is precisely what Lacan calls phallic *jouissance* and defines the masculine structure. A masculine structure is characterized by turning the Other into an *objet a*, and mistakenly thinking that the object can fully satisfy our desire. It is essential to keep in mind here, though, that phallic *jouissance* is not male in the sense that only men can experience it; it is experienced by both men and women and is defined as phallic insofar as it is characterized by failure.

FEMININITY

A feminine structure, on the other hand, is defined by a different rela-tionship to the Other and *jouissance* – what Lacan calls Other *jouissance*. The problem with talking about this Other *jouissance*, however, is that it cannot be spoken about. Speech is related to the symbolic order and is therefore phallic. If we could talk about this Other *jouissance* then it would, by definition, be *phallic*, as the symbolic order is phallic. Other *jouissance* is precisely something that one can experience but say nothing about and thus it is impossible to define. Now clearly this does not get us very far in an introduction to Lacan, so let us try to say what we can about this particular form of enjoyment. Fink points out that the notion of Other *jouissance* in Lacan is rather ambiguous and offers a number of possible readings: it could mean 'the *jouissance* the Other gets out of us', or 'our enjoyment of the Other', or 'our enjoyment as the Other' (2002: 38). All are possible readings of Lacan's formula. Fink also remains unclear why this Other *jouissance* should be defined as feminine (2002: 40).

The most well-known example of Other *jouissance* from seminar XX is of the statue 'The Ecstasy of Saint Teresa' by the Italian Baroque sculptor Lorenzo Bernini (1598–1680). This piece shows St Teresa swooning in ecstasy while pierced by an arrow from an angel poised above her. Lacan comments:

[I]t's like for Saint Teresa – you need but go to Rome and see the statue by Bernini to immediately understand that she's coming. There's no doubt about it. What is she getting off on? It is clear that the essential testimony of the mystics consists in saying that they experience it, but know nothing of it.

(1998 [1975]: 76)

This experience of unspeakable ecstasy is what Lacan calls Other or feminine *jouissance*. The idea of Other *jouissance* is seen to mark an advance over the phallocentrism of Freud, in that Other *jouissance* is 'more than' phallic *jouissance*; it is beyond the symbolic and the subject and therefore 'outside the unconscious' (Soler 2002: 107). Both men and women can experience phallic, or Other, *jouissance* and what defines whether or not a person has a masculine or a feminine structure is the type of *jouissance* they experience. There is one crucial difference, according to Lacan, between men and women, however, and that is that women can experience *both* forms of *jouissance* while with men it is either one or the other (see Fink 2002: 40–1). For Lacan, it is not the case that women are defined negatively in relation to men; a woman is *not* a man and therefore lacks something that men have – a penis. Rather, women have access to something more than men – a surplus *jouissance*.

THERE IS NO SUCH THING AS A SEXUAL RELATIONSHIP

Before turning to the example of courtly love, let me say something about one of Lacan's most perversely scandalous remarks about sexuality: there is no such thing as a sexual relationship. This formulation by Lacan is often understood, incorrectly I should add, in a similar vein to that of ex-US President Bill Clinton's equally scandalous remark that he did 'not have sexual relations' with Monica Lewinsky, a remark that nearly brought down his presidency. Bill Clinton took 'sexual relations' in this context to apply in a completely limited and literal sense to genital sex and thus, fortuitously for him, to exclude any other form of sexual activity. Lacan is not talking about sexual relations in this sense and is not suggesting that people do not have sexual relations with each other, of whatever form. Lacan is referring to a much more fundamental relationship than this – to the impossibility of a perfect sexual union between two people. Perhaps one of the most pervasive cultural fantasies we have today is of finding our perfect partner and of having a completely harmonious and sexually fulfilling relationship with our 'other half'. Indeed, many of the psychotherapies today are driven by the desire to achieve harmony and balance within families, between people and above all between the sexes. For Lacan this is a pernicious fantasy and the role of psychoanalysis is to reveal how any harmonious relationship is fundamentally impossible. It is precisely because masculinity and femininity represent two non-complementary structures, defined by different relationships to the Other, that there can be no such thing as a sexual relationship. What we do in any relationship is either try to turn the other into what we think we desire or turn ourselves into that which we think the other desires, but this can never exactly map onto the other's desire. In other words, the 'major problem of male and female subjects is that they do not relate to what their partners relate to in them' (Salecl 2002: 93). In a sense, we always miss what we aim at in the other and our desire remains unsatisfied. We can never be One, as Lacan says. It is this very asymmetry of masculinity and femininity in relation to the phallus and the *objet a* that means that there can be no such thing as a sexual relationship. According to Lacan, at least, masculine and feminine types of *jouissance* are *irreconcilable*. Let me now conclude this chapter with an example that Lacan takes from literature of the non-existence of women and the failure of the sexual relationship — that of the medieval tradition of courtly love poetry.

COURTLY LOVE

Courtly love is a tradition of lyric poetry that developed in Provence, southern France, in the late eleventh and early twelfth centuries and which spread throughout Western Europe in the Middle Ages. It embodies a whole philosophy of love and represents an elaborate code of behaviour which governs the relations between 'aristocratic' lovers, turning the more bodily and erotic aspects of love into a spiritual experience and the most elevated of passions. The courtly lover both idealizes and is idealized by his beloved and subjects himself entirely to her desires. However, there is an inherent impossibility, an obstacle to the fulfilment of love, in the very structure of courtly love. As it developed, courtly love often entailed the love between a single knight and a married woman. The most famous example of this in English literature is the love between Lancelot and Guinevere in King Arthur and the Knights of the Round Table. This love cannot be consummated in a physical sense and, if it is, disaster and death ensues. Courtly love therefore involves the agonies of unfulfilled love, but the lover remains true to his beloved, manifesting his honour and steadfastness in an unswerving adherence to the code of behaviour.

What Lacan finds of interest in these chivalric romances is, first, its symbolic aspect. Courtly love is 'a poetic exercise, a way of playing with a number of conventional, idealizing themes, which couldn't have any real concrete equivalent' (1992 [1986]: 148). Nevertheless, these symbolic conventions do have real concrete effects and even continue to organize 'contemporary man's sentimental attachments' (1992 [1986]: 148). First and foremost of these is 'the Lady', an impossibly idealized figure for which no real equivalent exists. Lacan writes:

> The object involved, the feminine object, is introduced oddly enough through the door of privation or of inaccessibility. Whatever the social position of him who functions in the role, the inaccessibility of the object is posited as a point of departure.
>
> (1992 [1986]: 149)

The Lady is the *objet a* (or *das Ding*, as Lacan calls it in this seminar) — that impossible object cause of desire that inaugurates the movement of desire itself. Crucially, then, she is not only unattainable but never existed in the first place; she is an idealized image for which there is no real equivalent. In *The Metastases of Enjoyment* Žižek points out that Lacan is careful here not to elevate the Lady to the status of a 'sublime' spiritualized object; she is rather an 'abstract character' – 'a cold, distanced, inhuman partner' who functions like an automaton or machine: '[T]he Lady is thus as far as possible from any kind of puri-fied spirituality: she functions as an inhuman partner in the sense of radical Otherness which is wholly incommensurable with our needs and desires' (1994: 90).

If the Lady of courtly love can be said to act as a mirror upon which the male lovers project their idealized images and fantasies, then this can only take place if the mirror is there already. This surface, the Lady, 'functions as a kind of black hole in reality, as a limit whose Beyond is inaccessible' (Žižek 1994: 91). In other words, she is exactly the kind of figure that one can have no empathetic relationship with whatsoever. She is that traumatic Otherness that Lacan designates as the Thing or the Real.

This is the structure of courtly love that continues to resonate with contemporary audiences and Žižek gives as an example of this Neil Jordan's 1993 film *The Crying Game*. *The Crying Game* centres on the 'love' affair between a member of the IRA, Fergus, on the run in London, and a beautiful hairdresser, Dil. While Fergus falls in love with Dil, she 'maintains an ambiguous ironic, sovereign distance towards him' (1994: 103). Eventually Dil gives way to Fergus's advances, but before they make love Dil retires to another room and changes into a semi-transparent nightgown. As the camera slowly follows Fergus's gaze and covetously moves down Dil's body, in one of the most startling moments in recent cinema, we suddenly see 'her' penis. Dil is a transvestite. Repulsed, Fergus pushes her away and throws up. After this failed sexual encounter their relationship is reversed and Dil becomes obsessively in love with Fergus, while he remains distant towards her. What we see here, therefore, is precisely the asymmetry that Lacan describes in all sexual relationships between 'what the lover sees in the loved one and what the loved one knows himself to be' (1994: 103). This is the inescapable deadlock of all sexual relationships, according to Lacan. Dil's love for Fergus is so absolute and unconditional that Fergus slowly overcomes his aversion to her. As the IRA tries to draw Fergus back into its activities, Dil shoots and kills Fergus's ex-lover and IRA operative, Jude. Fergus assumes responsibility for the killing and is imprisoned. The film ends with Dil visiting Fergus in prison, dressed once again as a provocatively seductive woman. They are now separated by the glass partition denying them any physical contact. For Žižek, this scenario encapsulates the impossibility of the sexual relationship.

SUMMARY

The issue of sexual difference is probably the most complicated and contested area of Lacanian theory. Lacan's thinking around sexual difference can be divided into two main phases. The first defines sexual difference in relation to the phallus: masculinity is defined in terms of having the phallus, while femininity is defined in terms of being the phallus. What is important in relation to this position is that the phallus is a 'fraud'; men cannot have the phallus any more than women can be the phallus. In the second phase of Lacan's work he concentrates much more on masculinity and femininity as structures that are open to both men and women. In this sense he moves away from the 'phallocentrism' of the earlier theory and explicitly attempts to account for women's desire. Thus, in late Lacan, masculinity and femininity are defined in relation to the type of *jouissance* one is able to attain. Masculinity is defined by a phallic *jouissance* that always fails, while femininity is defined by access to an Other unspeakable *jouissance* beyond phallic *jouissance*. In the section 'After Lacan' we will see how these ideas have been taken up within feminism and women's studies as well as the extensive criticisms against them.

AFTER LACAN

By the late 1970s psychoanalytic theory had largely fallen into disrepute within the universities. Psychoanalysis was particularly criticized for its reductionism, that is, reducing all social and cultural phenomena to psycho-sexual explanations. Whatever else one thinks about Lacan and his influence, the force of his 'return to Freud' has been to make us reconsider the relationship between the unconscious and culture, between the psyche and the social, in radically new and innovative ways. We will now briefly explore some of the most important work to have come out of Lacanian inspired studies, initially in the fields of social theory and feminism, then in literary and film studies.

SOCIAL THEORY

In 1964 Althusser published a ground-breaking essay entitled 'Freud and Lacan' (see 1984a). This essay ended decades of silence within 'orthodox' Marxist circles concerning psychoanalysis and marked a recognition that modern psychoanalytic ideas had a role to play in thinking about politics, ideology and subjectivity. According to Althusser, Marxism and psychoanalysis converge upon a specific problematic, that is, a particular *structure of mis-recognition*. For Marxism, this is the mis-recognition that individuals make history; for psychoanalysis, it is the subjects' mis-recognition of themselves as centred autonomous egos.

For Althusser, the pivotal link between these two moments of mis-recognition is ideology (1984b [1971]).

Previous conceptions of ideology within Marxism saw it as either 'false consciousness' or 'class affiliation'. Althusser argued, however, that ideology has nothing to do with questions of consciousness. Indeed, ideology is profoundly *unconscious* in the sense that it fails to work the moment we recognize it as ideological. Ideology is not a set of ideas or a system of beliefs; it is not a political programme through which subjects are indoctrinated. Ideology is rather a *system of representations*, a system of images, concepts and above all 'structures', which are *lived*. In short, ideology represents a subject's imaginary relation to their real conditions of existence. The importance of Althusser's work was to focus questions of ideology on representation *and the subject's constitution as an ideological subject within the system of representation*. This is also where it becomes important for literary, film and cultural studies generally because these disciplines are first and foremost concerned with systems of representation and hence questions of ideology.

Althusser's conception of ideology as an 'imaginary' relation to the 'real' conditions of existence clearly resonates with Lacanian theory. However, Marxism's primary interest lies with the representation of *social* reality, while psychoanalysis is concerned with the representation of *psychical* reality. Moreover, psychoanalysis involves a theory of representation that directly undermines the premise upon which Marxist theories of ideology operate, that is to say, that the represented (the object) always exists prior to the representation. Althusser's critics thus pointed out that psychoanalysis could not be combined with Marxism in the way he proposed.

THE SOCIAL-IDEOLOGICAL FANTASY

By the mid-1970s Althusserianism had collapsed under the weight of its own theoretical contradictions and limitations. However, Slavoj Žižek has continued to argue that Althusserianism is not the final, mistaken, word on the subject of ideology, but only a first step. According to Žižek, any properly psychoanalytic theory of ideology must take into account the constitutive role of fantasy, or what he calls the *social-ideological fantasy*. In *The Sublime Object of Ideology* (1989) Žižek argued that it is not the case that ideology is merely the false or illusory representation of reality, but rather that it is reality itself that is 'ideological'. The very idea of ideology as 'false' consciousness *presupposes* that we can attain a 'true' consciousness of reality, that is to say, that our representation of reality can be self-identical (or non-ideological) to that which it represents. What psychoanalysis teaches us through notions of unconscious desire and fantasy is that this is inherently impossible; that there will always be something that escapes – the *objet a* as remainder of the real. The function of the social-ideological fantasy is to mask the trauma that society itself is constituted by this inherent *lack*.

As we saw in Chapter 4, not only is the subject constituted through lack but so is the Other – the symbolic order. The recognition that the Other is lacking is a traumatic moment for the subject and the function of fantasy is to mask this trauma, and to make it bearable for the subject in some way. Lacan described this traumatic moment as our impossible encounter with the real. In terms of the social, Žižek identifies this traumatic moment as the fundamental *antagonism* at the root of all societies. We like to think of our society as naturally and harmoniously evolving over time and through the democratic consensus of the people. For Žižek this is not the case: *all* societies are founded upon a traumatic moment of social conflict and the social-ideological fantasy masks this constitutive antagonism. As Žižek writes, the 'ideological' is precisely '*a social reality whose very existence implies the non-knowledge of its participants as to its essence*' (1989: 21). That 'essence' is the moment of barbarity, conflict and antagonism that must be repressed if a society is to claim legitimacy as a 'natural', peaceful and democratically evolving state. Žižek has demonstrated this very well in his analysis of the conflicts in the Balkans throughout the 1990s. Many 'Western' commentators explained the eruption of so-called ethnic violence in the Balkans as the return of ancient 'tribal' conflicts and hatred suppressed by 50 years of communism. Žižek, on the other hand, suggests that what we see unfolding in the Balkans is nothing less than the eruption of the real into the symbolic. As the symbolic network of the former communist ideology and Yugoslav state disintegrated, we were confronted with the social antagonism constitutive of new 'democratic' societies (see Žižek 1993: 200–37). Furthermore, as these new micro-states gained independence, they began the process of elaborating new myths of national identity, but in order to do that they would first have to suppress the knowledge of the bloody conflict and ethnic cleansing of their moment of origin. Thus, the function of ideology, writes

Žižek, 'is not to offer us a point of escape from our reality but to offer us the social reality itself as an escape from some traumatic, real kernel' (1989: 45).

Žižek's conception of the social-ideological fantasy is indebted to Ernesto Laclau and Chantal Mouffe's influential work *Hegemony and Socialist Strategy* (1985). Drawing on the experience of the new social movements that have arisen since the 1960s – the women's movement, ecology, black consciousness, gay rights etc. – Laclau and Mouffe argued that politics in the traditional sense of party politics is finished and we must rethink the *political* as something that permeates every aspect of society and our lives. The political, argues Mouffe, 'cannot be restricted to a certain type of institution, or envisaged as consti-tuting a specific sphere or level of society. It must be conceived as a dimension that is inherent to every human society and that determines our ontological condition' (1993: 3). Where Laclau and Mouffe differed from other social theorists in the 1990s was their insistence, following Lacan, that both the subject and society are constituted through *lack*. What characterizes the struggles of the new social move-ments 'is precisely the multiplicity of subject positions which constitute a single agent' (Mouffe 1993: 12). In other words, we are not simply members of a particular social class, ethnic or gender group, but our subjectivity is criss-crossed by a number of different identities. At any given moment we occupy a number of intersecting subject positions inscribed through gender, race, sexual preference, professional status and familial position. The renewal of radical democratic politics, therefore, requires us to reject the notion of the individual as a self-contained unified entity existing independently of society and to conceive it as 'a site constituted by an ensemble of "subject positions", inscribed in a multiplicity of social relations, the member of many communities and participant in a plurality of collective forms of identification' (1993: 97).

Transposing Lacan's idea that 'there is no such thing as a sexual rela-tionship' to society Laclau and Mouffe argue that there 'can be no such thing as society'. From a Lacanian perspective there is no identity prior to its discursive constitution. All identity is equivalent to a 'differential position in a system of relations', or, to put it another way, 'all iden-tity is discursive' and based on difference (Laclau 1990: 217). Social identity, just as much as individual identity, cannot be said to be based upon some ultimate self-identity with its object; on the capacity of society to fully constitute itself, to be, if you like, objectively given and knowable. There is always something in excess; something that slips away from the attempt to ideologically fix it. The social, in other words, is an 'impossible object'.

The implications of Lacanian psychoanalysis for social theory and our understanding of democracy have been more fully developed by Yannis Stavrakakis in *Lacan and the Political* (1999). These ideas have also influenced post-colonial theory, especially through the work of Homi Bhabha (see *The Location of Culture* (1994)). As we will see below, the idea of 'subject positioning' was to have a significant influence on the psychoanalytic film theory associated with the journal *Screen*. More recently, Lacanian psychoanalysis has been used to counter the turn to ethics in social and cultural theory and especially the ethics of difference or otherness (see Badiou 2002).

FEMINISM

The Lacanian account of sexual difference has had a far-reaching, albeit rather ambivalent, impact on Anglo-American feminism. If political theory is concerned to give an account of how social norms are successfully internalized by subjects, what a psychoanalytic understanding of the unconscious forces us to recognize is how this internalization necessarily fails. For Jacqueline Rose (1996c), it is this resistance to any stable identity at the heart of psychic life that creates a particular affinity between psychoanalysis and feminism. The inherent instability of identity undermines traditional conceptions of political identity and solidarity, but also opens up the possibility for non-normative theories of subjectivity. The implications for feminist politics of this encounter with Lacanian psychoanalysis would be most fully explored in the pages of the journal *m/f* (see Adams and Cowie 1990).

In its opening editorial *m/f* declared itself to be a journal committed to the 'women's movement', but at the same time against the essentialism to which many parts of that movement subscribed. Thus, the journal set out to systematically interrogate the categories of gender and sexual difference and to show how these identities are not pregiven but produced through complex sets of social and psychic investments. For example, the category of the 'feminine' is not something determined by one's anatomy but, as Lacan showed, the result of psychic processes that cannot be accounted for by either biology or social processes. To suggest that women's unequal position within society can be explained simply through sexual difference or gender is to impute a fixed and unchanging essence to the notion of the feminine which psychoanalysis reveals as untenable. The category 'woman' cannot be said to exist, as there is no inherent feminine nature or fixed identity to which the term applies. One result of Lacanian feminism, therefore, was to dissolve the boundary between men and women, on which the women's movement was founded:

> If there is no one subject position there can be no *sexual division* between feminine subjects and male subjects, for sexual division always requires full subjects already sexually differentiated, that is organized into two unitary groups.
>
> (Adams and Cowie 1990: 29)

As there is no innate sexual division between men and women based on fixed identities, what is at stake for feminism is the organization of *sexual difference* through social practices and within social relations. The legacy of *m/f*, as Chantal Mouffe succinctly puts it, was to make 'a general theory of women's oppression a thing of the past' (1990: 4). For other feminists this has also been the main problem with Lacanianism and the deconstruction of 'woman' as a category. If the notion of the woman no longer exists, then on what grounds can a feminist politics be elaborated? A more critical appropriation of Lacan was developed though the work of Luce Irigaray and Julia Kristeva.

IRIGARAY AND THE FEMININE IMAGINARY

Luce Irigaray trained as a psychoanalyst with Lacan's *École Freudienne*, but with the publication of her doctoral thesis *Speculum of the Other Woman* in 1974 (see 1985a) she was expelled. Margaret Whitford argues that Irigaray is not so much a Lacanian feminist as a post-Lacanian, in the sense that she is proposing to change the symbolic order through the articulation of a feminine imaginary. Irigaray is both indebted to Lacanian psychoanalysis and highly critical of it. In 'The Poverty of Psychoanalysis' she develops three main lines of critique: first, both psychoanalysis and its attitude towards women are historically determined, as the discipline does not recognize this it is inherently phallocentric; second, the symbolic order rests on an unacknowledged incorporation of the mother; and finally, psycho-analysis is governed by and perpetuates dominant cultural fantasies, especially with respect to women, and as it does not acknowledge these fantasies we can see repression and defences at work within the theory itself (Whitford 1991: 31). In short, Irigaray argues that the feminine is the unacknowledged unconscious of psychoanalysis and of Western culture in general.

The problem for Irigaray is how to define the feminine without being locked into patriarchal frameworks. The psychoanalytic under-standing of sexual difference is based on the *visibility* of difference and therefore the feminine is always perceived as the absence or negation of the masculine norm. Consequently, women are excluded from representation. Drawing on the work of the social theorist and critic of Lacan, Cornelius Castoriadis (1987), Irigaray develops a more posi-tive and creative conception of the imaginary. Unlike the Lacanian realm of illusion and misrecognition, the imaginary for Castoriadis and Irigaray is unconscious fantasy. It is also, for Irigaray, *sexed* and thus she distinguishes between the male imaginary of identity, rational-ity and phallocentrism and the female imaginary of multiplicity, fluidity and flux. Irigaray is suggesting not that women are irrational but rather that rationality itself has been historically constructed in such a way that the feminine is inevitably repressed. For Irigaray, therefore, the feminine is something that has to be created and given symbolic form and she proposes a strategy for doing this through 'speaking (as) woman'. Whitford (1991) suggests that there are at least three senses in which we can understand this strategy: first, the feminine becomes a kind of natural and unmediated expression, involving a regression to the pre-Oedipal relation to the body and mother; second, it is the articulation of the unconscious; and third, it is a specific psychic struc-ture. What is important to keep in mind here is that Irigaray is trying to imagine the unimaginable and to think the beyond of sexual differ-ence. In a sense the feminine imaginary is very close to the Lacanian real. Irigaray, however, gives it a positive content and says that it can be articulated.

In *This Sex Which is Not One* (1985b [1977]) Irigaray opposes the singularity of the phallus as the signifier of sexual difference with the multiplicity of feminine sexuality – the vagina, lips, clitoris, breasts and uterus. The duality of the lips – two not one, genitals and mouth – come to symbolize feminine sexuality. The Lacanian response to

Irigaray's work is that she is an essentialist in the sense that the feminine represents some kind of pre-given libido and also that she rejects symbolic castration. Whitford (1991) argues, however, that the Lacanian critique misses the point as Irigaray is not primarily concerned with the drives but with the symbolic and representation. Irigaray sees Lacan as a symbolic determinist and the point is not to work within the symbolic as it is, but to change the structure itself, that is to say, to find ways in which the feminine can be represented other than as lack or a 'hole'. It is this aspect of her work that has found particular resonance within feminist cultural studies.

KRISTEVA AND THE SEMIOTIC

The second major influence from French feminism has been Julia Kristeva and especially her early work on the semiotic. In the same year that Irigaray published *Speculum*, Kristeva published *Revolution in Poetic Language* (1984 [1974]). Kristeva defines the 'signifying process' as a dialectical interaction between the 'semiotic' and the 'symbolic'. The semiotic and the symbolic are sometimes taken to be a reworking of Lacan's distinction between the imaginary and the symbolic, but the semiotic in fact has many of the properties of the real. The symbolic, for Kristeva, is the formal structure of language, while the semiotic is linked to the pre-Oedipal primary processes. The semiotic is thus linked to the body and the drive which Kristeva locates in the *chora* (usually translated from the Greek as enclosed space or womb). The *chora* is not a fixed place, however, but an endless movement and pulsation beneath the symbolic. The semiotic functions as a disruptive pressure on the symbolic and can be traced through the gaps in language, the tendency to meaninglessness and laughter. In *Revolution in Poetic Language* Kristeva identifies this kind of language with avant-garde poetry and literature.

Kristeva's views on feminism and women are almost as outrageous as Lacan's. 'To believe that one "is a woman",' writes Kristeva, 'is almost as absurd and obscurantist as to believe that one "is a man"' (quoted in Moi 1985: 163). For Kristeva, one cannot *be* a woman because 'woman' is a social construct. Kristeva defines 'woman' as that which is outside representation; that which cannot be spoken. Unlike Irigaray, though, she stresses the negativity of women's position in relation to the phallocentric order rather than attempting to articulate positive representations of the feminine. What women share with other oppressed groups within society is a position of marginality with respect to the dominant ideology and language. It is in this respect that women and other marginal groups are associated with the semiotic, as that which is outside the dominant discourse and marginal to it.

QUEERING THE PHALLUS

The Lacanian account of sexual difference has also been criticized from the perspective of Queer theory. In *Bodies That Matter* Judith Butler (1993) challenges the psychoanalytic account of sexual difference on grounds that it is based upon the normalization of heterosexual couples and does not take into account other forms of sexual relationship. Drawing on Michel Foucault's (1926–84) conception of discourse, Butler argues that the psyche and the social must be seen as a continuum and that sexual difference itself is discursively constituted. In an impressive piece of textual analysis Butler reads Lacan's 'The Mirror Stage' and 'The Signification of the Phallus' against Freud's paper 'On Narcissism' to highlight the inherent instability and contingency of the psychoanalytic conception of the phallus. What is important here is that Butler rejects not the notion of the phallus per se but its privileged status within psychoanalytic theory. What we can see in Freud's text, argues Butler, is a certain ambivalence at the very heart of his theory insofar as 'the phallus belongs to no body part, but is fundamentally transferable and is at least within this text, the very principle of erotogenic transferability' (1993: 62). Paradoxically, therefore, the lesson of Freudian psychoanalysis is not that there is a single privileged signifier but rather that anatomy cannot provide the stable referent that anchors the signifying chain. According to Butler, our bodies cannot be taken for granted because they are always acquired. Butler is not suggesting here that our bodies are simply linguistic constructs, but insofar as our bodies bear on language they can never fully escape from the process through which they are signified.

From this perspective Butler takes to task Lacan for his conception of the body in the mirror stage. There are two fundamental problems with Lacan's account of the body as an imaginary function. First, the schema is essentially masculine and becomes the basis for a more far-reaching masculine epistemology within Lacanian discourse. Second, the idealization of the body in 'The Mirror Stage' as the centre of control is then rearticulated in 'The Signification of the Phallus' in the form of the phallus as that which controls signification (1993: 73). For Butler, however, to claim that the phallus has a privileged status in relation to other signifiers *performatively* produces the effects of that privilege. In other words, the phallus acquires its privileged status simply because we say it does. Following Irigaray, Butler argues that there is not one imaginary schema, but alternative schemes – female, male, heterosexual, bisexual, homosexual etc. – and in each of these schemes the phallus will function differently. More specifically, Butler argues for a lesbian phallus that depends on its displacement as a signifier from the penis to other body parts and thus undermines psychoanalysis' phallocentric view of castration anxiety and penis envy. The lesbian phallus constitutes an 'ambivalent site of identification and desire that is significantly different from the scene of normative heterosexuality to which it is related' (1993: 85). In this sense the lesbian phallus is a transferable fantasy, it is not related to a single body part and is not a 'real' thing. The phallus thus loses its sense of being the privileged signifier and becomes merely one signifier among others; it has neither the status of the original signifier nor the unspeakable outside of discourse. To speak of the lesbian phallus is to offer an alternative imaginary and to break with the 'hetero-normative' account of sexual difference. However, in order to do this, suggests Butler, we need not replace the phallus with a new body part but displace the dominant symbolism of heterosexual difference and release alternative imaginary schema for constituting sites of erotogenic pleasure.

Butler's work has been extremely influential in providing a critique of the phallocentrism and 'hetero-normative' bias of psychoanalysis, but her view of the discursive construction of sex has also been challenged from within Lacanian circles (see Copjec 1994a). Moreover, her critique of the body in Lacanian psychoanalysis focuses on only one aspect of the body – the imaginary body of the mirror phase – whereas the body functions differently in each of Lacan's three registers. For Lacan 'the body is a reality' (Soler 1995b: 7), but he does not mean by this that the body is pre-given. According to Lacan, we are not born with a body as such but we rather acquire our bodies as Butler suggests. Lacan first approached the body through the notion of the fragmented body of the mirror stage – the bodily experience of the infant as it stares at the unified image in the mirror. In the 1950s he radically changed his conception of the body and suggested that there was a fundamental breach between the body and its image. His focus thus turned to the body as it was represented in the symbolic by the signifier or the signified body. In the final phase of his career Lacan turned his attention much more to the notion of the body as real, that is to say, the body as unsymbolizable. For Lacan, the body is real not because it is pre-symbolic but insofar as 'it is impossible to apprehend by means of the signifier' (Soler 1995b: 30). The full impact of Lacan's conception of the body has yet to be taken up by cultural studies.

LITERARY THEORY

Classical psychoanalytic criticism or applied psychoanalysis has focused on the 'content' of literary works and the psychology of the author or characters. Lacan's readings focus on the 'form' and structure of texts. For Lacan, literature is exemplary of psychic structures rather than the content of any individual unconscious. In *Literature and Psychoanalysis* (first published as a volume of *Yale French Studies* in 1977 and reprinted as a book in 1982) Shoshana Felman gives an extraordinary demonstration of Lacanian psychoanalytic reading. Traditionally psychoanalysis has claimed the position of the master discourse, while literature is assigned the subordinate position as a set of texts in need of interpretation. For Felman, though, literature is not a separate discourse outside psychoanalysis, but since its inception – that is, Freud's encounter with Sophocles' *Oedipus Rex* – literature provides the language through which psychoanalysis can speak its concepts and its truths. Felman, therefore, suggests that we should replace the notion of *application* with one of *implication*.

As an example of what this might mean in practice we can take Felman's own exhaustive reading of Henry James's sensational ghost story *The Turn of the Screw*. James's little 'potboiler', as he called it, tells the story of a governess who takes charge of two young children, Miles and Flora, in a remote country house. The children's guardian is absent, having no interest in their care, and the governess is assisted by a housekeeper, Mrs Grose. Very soon after arriving at the house the governess begins to see the ghosts of a man and a woman, who she learns from Mrs Grose are the previous governess and her lover, the stableman, who both died in mysterious circumstances. The governess believes that the children are in secret communication with the ghosts but no one else appears to see them. Eventually the governess sends Flora away with Mrs Grose and forces Miles to confront the ghosts with tragic consequences. James's story met with a storm of outrage when it was first published, with critics describing it as 'evil' and 'repulsive' (see Felman 1982: 96–7). This scandal was to be repeated some 30 years later when Edmund Wilson published a 'Freudian reading' of the text (1965). Wilson argued that *The Turn of the Screw* was not actually a ghost story at all but a case study in neurosis. Wilson's article was extensively criticized for its Freudian reductionism and Wilson subsequently revised it a number of times, but each time retaining his psychological explanation. The critical debate over this short story revolves around the question of whether or not the ghosts actually exist and therefore whether the governess is trying to save the children from evil or whether she is quite simply mad.

What is of interest to Felman is not which of the various interpretations is correct, but the structure of the debate itself, the way in which James's tale caused such a sensation upon publication and its repetition in the subsequent history of its criticism. If Wilson's Freudian reading of the text is so far off the mark, then why have so many subsequent critics felt the necessity to refute it and, for that matter, why did Wilson continually respond to their criticisms? What can be said to be psychoanalytic here is not the content of the story – whether or not the children were introduced to forbidden sexual knowledge by the former governess and her lover or, indeed, sexually abused by them – but the structure of repetition that the text enacts. The text is a signifier that insists on expression, but at the same time continually undercuts any stable or fixed meaning. The reader cannot settle on a final definitive interpretation of this text, because its very structure resists such a possibility. The reader can either believe the governess and thus naively believe in ghosts like the housekeeper or be sceptical about the existence of ghosts and thus be neurotic like the governess. These are the two possible reading positions that the text offers us and are continually repeated in the history of its criticism, neither of them being particularly satisfying.

What Felman demonstrates in this virtuoso reading is that these two positions are inscribed within the text itself, and that the critic and reader are caught up in them just as much as the characters in the story. She is concerned, therefore, not with 'what' the text means, but with 'how' it achieves certain effects and how the reader's desire is caught up in a chain of signification. Elizabeth Wright (1998) highlights a number of unanswered questions concerning Felman's reading, which centre on the issue of *transference*; both the transference of the author and the transference of the critic/reader.

TRANSFERENCE AND THE TEXT

One of the most fruitful developments in contemporary psychoanalytic criticism has been the use of 'transference' to account for the relationship between readers and texts. What psychoanalysis calls 'transference' is a form of resistance and it involves the unconscious displacement through time and place of a past relationship into the present. That is to say, previous infantile or early relationships will be displaced and in some sense restaged in the analytic situation, through the relationship between the analysand and analyst. The transference is always ambivalent; it is both a relationship of love (positive-transference) and hate (negative-transference) and thus inherently unstable. The transference involves strong feelings being invoked in the relationship between analyst and analysand, which cannot be accounted for by the reality of the situation. In seminar XI Lacan reformulated Freud's notion of transference to include what he called 'the subject supposed to know'. The analysand places the analyst in the position of an all-knowing expert who has all the answers and thus idealizes their analyst. The emphasis in Lacan's formulation, however, should be placed not on the 'knowing' but on the 'supposed'; the analyst does not know and does not have all the answers. This formulation of the transference has important implications for the relationship between reader and text, because as readers we assume that the text 'knows', and that the text has all the answers. What Lacan's understanding of the transference points to is the fact that we must see the meaning of any given text not within the text itself but as a reconstruction between reader and text.

In 'The Idea of a Psychoanalytic Literary Criticism' (1987) Peter Brooks argues that the use of psychoanalysis as a model for literary theory is not arbitrary because there is a direct correspondence between the psychoanalytic conception of the mind and literature. Both psychoanalysis and literature converge on the question of the subject and representation. This is also where the transference arises. Transference 'is a realm of as-if, where affects from the past become invested in the present'; in other words, transference is 'a representation of the past' (1987: 9). The transference creates an intermediate region that is neither past nor present, neither inside nor outside, neither fiction nor reality. In short, transference is textual in nature. All texts have an implicit or implied addressee – a reader. The text is, therefore, inherently dialogic in structure. We intervene in the text through the very act of reading, just as much as the text guides and manipulates our desires as readers. The process of reading then is in a sense both transferential and counter-transferential. The usefulness of this comparison between reading and transference is that it illuminates the complex encounter between reader and text which takes place in an artificial space – a symbolic space – that is at the same time the place of real investments of desire. What motivates us to read and study literature is really a very intense desire – a love of literature – that is played out in the dynamics between reader and text.

FILM THEORY

In Chapter 1 we looked at the influence of Lacan on film theory. Apparatus, or *Screen*, theory, as it was known, saw cinema as essentially a machine that ideologically constructed spectators. It was also exemplary of what Constance Penley (1989) rather neatly calls a *bachelor machine*, that is to say, a self-enclosed signifying system that excludes feminine identity. The apparatus theorists worked with the idea of cinema as a voyeuristic and fetishistic structure. Freud's account of voyeurism and fetishism only has meaning in relation to the question of sexual difference, but apparatus theorists attributed it to cinema spectators in general. What we see here, therefore, is a prime example of 'disavowal' itself – the disavowal of sexual difference and the exclusion of feminine identity in contemporary film theory. What was required was a much more subtle and intricate reading of the psychoanalytic insights into vision and subjectivity, especially into the notion of the gaze (Copjec 1994b).

THE EYE AND THE GAZE

In seminar XI Lacan developed Merleau-Ponty's idea of a pre-existing gaze that stares at us from the outside. For Merleau-Ponty this gaze emanates from an all-seeing transcendental subject, but for Lacan no such subject exists. According to Lacan, we are not primarily conscious subjects viewing the world, but rather we are always-already 'beings that are looked at' (1979 [1973]: 74–5). There is a fundamental separation between the eye and the gaze. While 'I' see from only one point, I am looked at from all sides. There is a gaze that pre-exists my subjective view – an all-*seeing* to which I am subjected. Žižek summarizes these notions well:

> the eye viewing the object is on the side of the subject, while the gaze is on the side of the object. When I look at an object, the object is always already gazing at me, and from a point at which I cannot see it.
>
> (1992: 109)

A good example of how the gaze can be utilized in film is given by Žižek (1992) in his analysis of Hitchcock's *Psycho* (1960). Towards the end of the film Lilah climbs the hill to the old house where Norman and his 'mother' live. Here Hitchcock's film technique alternates between the objective shot of Lilah climbing the hill and her subjective view of the house. Žižek suggests that Hitchcock's editing style allows for two possible kinds of shot but also forbids two other kinds. With Hitchcock we either get 'the objective shot of the person approaching a Thing' or 'the subjective shot presenting the Thing as the person sees it' (1992: 117), but we never get the objective shot of the Thing or the subjective shot of the person from the position of the Thing. In this sequence from *Psycho* we only ever see the house from Lilah's point of view; there is no neutral, 'objective' shot of the house itself, as this would dispel the mystery and foreboding that surrounds the unknown Thing. The sense of uncanniness would also be lost if Hitchcock 'subjectivized' the Thing by providing subjective shots from inside the house itself; for instance, the standard shot of a trembling hand pulling back a curtain and looking at the figure coming up the hill. We only see the house from Lilah's point of view, but it is *the house that gazes back at Lilah*. Lilah approaches the house but she cannot see it from the position that it gazes back at her.

Lacan's conception of the gaze also has further implications for film theory. It is in the split between the eye and the gaze that the drive is manifested in the visual field (1979 [1973]: 73). In other words, the gaze is not something that can be seen, as by its very nature it is that which escapes the field of vision, but it is something that can be represented in the form of the *objet a*. Lacan's theory of the gaze, therefore, directs us to the function of the *objet a* and fantasy in film.

FILM AS FANTASY

Fantasy is never purely a private affair; fantasies circulate in the public domain through such media as film, literature and television. Fantasy is the 'privileged terrain on which social reality and the unconscious are engaged in a figuring which intertwines them both' (Cowie 1990: 164). Fantasy is the *mise-en-scène* of desire. Mise-en-scène refers to the setting or arrangement of everything within the film frame; in other words, the lighting, costumes, properties, as well as the positioning of characters and properties within the frame. It is this notion that provides the link between fantasy, as the staging of desire, and film, as the setting for the desire of the spectator. Film provides a complex set of positions and potential relations through which spectators can play out their desire. The role of narrative is central here, in that it provides recognizable structures and coherence at the level of both fantasy and film. The pleasure we derive from fantasy is not so much a consequence of it achieving its aim, its object; but rather how the desire is able to play itself out through the narrative structure.

Cowie (1997) provides a detailed analysis of the different levels of fantasy at work in *Now, Voyager* (1943) that we can only briefly touch upon here. The film tells the story of Charlotte Vale (Bette Davis), the spinster daughter of a wealthy family who suffers a nervous breakdown at the hands of her domineering mother. Against the wishes of her mother, Charlotte is sent to a sanatorium, where she recovers, and as a reward she goes on an ocean cruise. During the cruise Charlotte falls in love with a married man, Jerry Durrance (Paul Henreid). They part after three days and Charlotte returns home to her mother. Back at home Charlotte's mother resumes her previous domineering behaviour. At first Charlotte succumbs, but eventually she resists her mother's pressure and her new self is allowed to prevail. Charlotte gets engaged to a fellow wealthy Bostonian, but when she receives a gift from her ex-lover, she breaks off the engagement causing a row with her mother that results in a fatal heart attack. Feeling guilty, Charlotte returns to the sanatorium where she meets Jerry's daughter, Tina, also the victim of an uncaring mother. The film concludes with

Charlotte and Tina living happily together as mother and daughter. Jerry visits the house and says he cannot allow Charlotte to sacrifice her life for him, but Charlotte responds that they can be together through the child if not in person.

Cowie (1997) shows how there are a number of different levels of fantasy at work here, and particularly how the contingent day-dream or wish-fulfilment fantasies are linked to a more primal, original, fantasy. First, at what we might call a surface textual level, there is the desire for recognition: Charlotte's desire to be recognized by her doctor as a person of worth, the triumph of the cruise voyage and her independence from her mother. More importantly, there is the desire for the love of a man she experiences on the cruise. Charlotte's engagement, on the other hand, provides a different kind of wish-fulfilment fantasy, in the sense that her fiancé had previously rejected her and now, after her return from the sanatorium, she is able to reject him and remain true to her 'absolute' love that remains forever out of reach. The final scenes of the film, therefore, could be said to play out the scenario of 'a secret love, passionate and fulfilling as "reality" could never be' (Cowie 1997: 146). At a deeper level, however, there is a more fundamental fantasy at work here, which revolves around the role of the mother. Charlotte displaces her mother, but in doing so she becomes everything that the mother never was for her or for Tina. Rather strangely Charlotte's desire for a child and motherhood is fulfilled without her having sex. According to Cowie, there is a clear Oedipal trajectory played out in the film, but with an important twist. Charlotte transfers her desire from her mother as the first love object but *not* on to the father. Charlotte manages to obtain a child and evict the father at the same time. Thus, the film does not follow the usual Hollywood trajectory of ending with the happy couple Charlotte and Jerry, but it ends instead with the alternative couple Charlotte and Tina. The film turns back upon itself, refusing the Oedipal trajectory by focusing on the mother/child relationship and the desire for the 'good' mother. What is important to notice here is that this is a case of psychoanalysing not the characters of the film, but part of the narrative structure itself. The film presents a series of wish-fulfilment fantasies, but at a deeper level we find an Oedipal primal fantasy of origins – how children can be born without having sex. The subject of this fantasy is not Charlotte, but the spectator who is caught up in the film's narration and plays out their own desire through it.

The focus of Lacanian psychoanalytic film theory today has shifted from the early preoccupation with the mirror stage and subject positioning to an appreciation of the later work of Lacan on the real, fantasy and the gaze. Contrary to much of the early psychoanalytic film theory this new work also produces startling readings of individual films. See in this respect the edited volumes *Gaze and Voice as Love Objects* by Salecl and Žižek (1996) and, more recently, *Lacan and Contemporary Film* by McGowan and Kunkle (2004).

SUMMARY

The unconscious and human desire permeate our representations and create a permanent state of instability and disruption at the very heart of our culture. The continuing relevance and value of Lacanian psychoanalysis is to hold open that space and to refuse the 'ideological' closure of a unified, harmonious, conflict-free subject or society as well as to analyse the ways in which desire manifests itself through cultural texts.

FURTHER READING

WORKS BY JACQUES LACAN

Lacan only published one book in his lifetime – *Écrits* (Paris: Editions du Seuil, 1966), and oversaw the editing of the first of his seminars – *Le Séminaire de Jacques Lacan, Livre XI: Les quatre concepts fondamentaux de la psychanalyse* (Paris: Editions du Seuil, 1973). The English translation, *Écrits: A Selection* by Alan Sheridan (London: Tavistock Publications, 1977), contains many of the key texts we have discussed in the preceding chapters: 'The Mirror Stage', 'The Rome Discourse', 'The Agency of the Letter in the Unconscious', 'The Meaning of the Phallus' and 'The Subversion of the Subject and the Dialectic of Desire', but it still only consists of one-third of the French edition. A new translation of this selection has recently been produced by Bruce Fink (*Écrits: A Selection*, New York: Norton, 2002) but his translation of the complete *Écrits* is still awaited. Fink's extensively annotated translations will undoubtedly become the standard authoritative texts of Lacan in the coming years but as this is not yet the case all references in this introduction are to the Sheridan edition.

Lacan was 65 years old when he published *Écrits* and it is not an introductory text but the summation of a lifetime's teaching and clinical practice. Each paper contains a multiplicity of allusions and references that need to be unpacked, if we are to begin understanding

Lacan's ideas. 'The Mirror Stage', for example, is only seven pages long, while 'The Signification of the Phallus' is just nine, but each of these papers has generated volumes of explication, critique and applications. I would suggest that a better way to read Lacan is through the seminars and the accompanying *Readings* published by SUNY Press (see 'Works on Jacques Lacan' below). The seminar is unquestionably an unusual reading experience. Each seminar contains approximately 25 presentations from the fortnightly seminar (although they get shorter as Lacan reduces his theory to a set of mathematical formulas in his final years). While each presentation is supposed to pick up and follow on from the week before, the connections can often be tenuous. Unlike the *Écrits*, the seminars are not difficult to read, but it can still be hard to follow the train of associations and links that Lacan makes. Usually, though, in a performative flourish Lacan will pull the whole presentation together in the final moments and provide a startlingly clear and understandable formulation of what he has been talking about. So, however bewildering the seminar might seem, it is always worth following it through. From the currently published seminars a good place to start would be *Seminars II*, *VII* and *XI*.

―――― (1975) *Le Séminaire, Livre I: Les écrits techniques de Freud*, Paris: Editions du Seuil (English version, *The Seminar of Jacques Lacan, Book I: Freud's Papers on Technique, 1953–1954*, ed. J.-A. Miller, trans. J. Forrester, Cambridge: Cambridge University Press, 1988).

This seminar is perhaps the least interesting to students of the humanities and social sciences, as it concerns questions of psychoanalytic technique. Freud's papers on technique (vol. 12 of the Standard Edition) were left out of the Penguin Freud Library, as they are explicitly addressed to analysts. Lacan's seminar looks at questions of resistance and defence mechanisms, repression and desire, as well as transference. *Book I* also contains his early formulation of the imaginary and his critique of the Object Relations School of psychoanalysis.

―――― (1978) *Le Séminaire, Livre II: Le moi dans la théorie de Freud et dans la technique de la psychanalyse, 1954–1955*, Paris: Editions du Seuil (English version, *The Seminar of Jacques Lacan, Book II: The Ego in Freud's Theory and in the Technique of Psychoanalysis, 1954–1955*, ed. J.-A. Miller, trans. S. Tomaselli, Cambridge: Cambridge University Press, 1988).

The second seminar is a study of Freud's 'Beyond the Pleasure Principle' – a central text throughout Lacan's career. This seminar contains Lacan's early formulation of the symbolic order and the circuit of discourse. Lacan explores the notion of repetition in Freud and how the subject is constituted within the chain of signification. This seminar also contains an early short version of *The Purloined Letter* paper and some rather strange reflections on language and cybernetics.

—— (1981) *Le Séminaire, Livre III: Les psychoses*, Paris: Editions du Seuil (English version, *The Seminar of Jacques Lacan, Book III: The Psychoses 1955–1956*, ed. J.-A. Miller, trans. R. Grigg, London: Routledge, 1993).

Only the first half of this seminar is explicitly concerned with questions of psychosis and psychotic phenomenon. The second half looks at hysteria, the relationship between the signifier and the signified and finally issues of metaphor and metonymy. The seminar also contains early formulations of the Name-of-the-Father and the phallus.

—— (1986) *Le Séminaire, Livre VII: L'ethique de la psychanalyse, 1959–1960*, Paris: Editions du Seuil (English version, *The Seminar of Jacques Lacan, Book VII: The Ethics of Psychoanalysis 1959–1960*, ed. J.-A. Miller, trans. D. Porter, London: Routledge, 1992).

This seminar has been crucial for the wider dissemination of Lacanian ideas in the humanities and social sciences and it provides a constant reference point for Žižek as well as feminist critics. The seminar contains Lacan's only reference to *das Ding* (the Thing) as well as his reflections on sublimation and *jouissance*. The seminar is probably most well known though for Lacan's discussion of Sophocles' ancient Greek tragedy *Antigone*, where he elaborates one of his most influential definitions of the ethical act – 'not to give way on one's desire' – and feminine sexuality in relation to courtly love poetry. This seminar is a very accessible and essential reading.

—— (1973) *Le Séminaire de Jacques Lacan, Livre XI: Les quatre concepts fondamentaux de la psychanalyse*, Paris: Editions du Seuil (English version, *The Four Fundamental Concepts of Psycho-Analysis*, ed. J.-A. Miller, trans. A. Sheridan, London: Hogarth Press, 1977; reprinted Harmondsworth: Penguin Books, 1979, and with a new introduction by D. Macey, 1994).

This is a dense and difficult text to read, but it is unquestionably the pivotal seminar of Lacan's career and one that you will read over and over again. It is an immensely rich text, packed with ideas and formulations that Lacan will return to throughout the second half of his career. Lacan differentiates his work from orthodox Freudianism on some of the fundamental concepts of psychoanalysis, the unconscious, transference, the drive and the subject. He also begins to reformulate many of his earlier concepts and to elaborate what we now recognize as a specifically Lacanian theory of psychoanalysis. Most importantly, Lacan stresses the centrality of the 'drive' as the distinguishing feature of psychoanalysis. He reformulates his understanding of the subject from the subject of the signifier to the subject of the drive and replaces some of the linguistic terminology, such as metaphor and metonymy, with alienation and separation. Lacan also develops the *objet petit a* – as the object cause of desire and remainder of the real – in relation to the split between the eye and the gaze. Finally, the seminar develops a notion of transference as a relation to 'the subject supposed to know'.

—— (1975) *Le Séminaire, Livre XX: Encore, 1972–1973*, Paris: Editions du Seuil (English version, *The Seminar of Jacques Lacan, Book XX: Encore, On Feminine Sexuality, The Limits of Love and Knowledge 1972–1973*, ed. J.-A. Miller, trans. B. Fink, New York: Norton, 1998).

Seminar XX is Lacan's major work on feminine sexuality. In particular he explores the question of feminine desire that was absent from his earlier theory of the phallus. It is a short seminar with only 11 presentations and many of these are rather enigmatic and aphoristic, if they are not read in relation to the discussion of courtly love in *Seminar VII* and the formulation of *jouissance* and drive in *Seminar XI*. *Seminar XX* develops the idea that the 'woman does not exist' and that she is 'not-whole', but also goes beyond discussions of feminine sexuality to consider the relationship between *jouissance* and love and the idea of *jouissance* as the ultimate limit of human knowledge.

WORKS ON JACQUES LACAN

As I indicated above, the best way into Lacan today is through a series of *Readings* to the main seminars, which have come out over the last few years. These volumes should not be read in place of the seminars but in parallel to them, especially because they are not 'readers' in the sense that they give a systematic explication of the seminars, but rather collections of essays that elaborate the central themes of each seminar. The series began as the publication of seminars given, in English, in

Paris by prominent Lacanian analysts to counter what the Parisians saw as the misreading of Lacan in the Anglo-American academy. As such, one should keep in mind that these collections attempt to establish an 'orthodox' reading of Lacan and often involve a certain retrospective formalization of Lacan from the perspective of his later work. This being said, the collections contain some of the most concise and accessible – as well as a few obscure ones – introductions to Lacanian concepts currently available in English.

Feldstein, R., Fink, B. and Jaanus, M. (eds) (1995) *Reading Seminar XI: Lacan's Four Fundamental Concepts of Psychoanalysis*, New York: SUNY Press.

This volume begins with a contextualizing introduction by Miller and concluding with Lacan's (1964) article 'The Position of the Unconscious' (see 1995). Eric Laurent's papers on 'alienation and separation' can be a bit confusing at times, if one is not familiar with some Lacanian concepts, but are useful introductions. Soler's two contributions on the 'subject and Other' are as succinct and accessible as all her writing. Marie-Hélène Brousse's contributions on the drive will also help to clarify this difficult concept. *Reading Seminar XI* also has a strong cultural emphasis. The section on 'The Gaze and Object *a*' has a good introduction to the concepts by Antonio Quinet followed by a series of applications of the concepts by Richard Feldstein (literature), Hanjo Berressem and Robert Samuels (art) and Žižek (film). The clinical section is restricted to two papers by Anne Dunand on the very controversial issue of the 'end' of analysis.

Feldstein, R., Fink, B. and Jaanus, M. (eds) (1996) *Reading Seminars I and II: Lacan's Return to Freud*, New York: SUNY Press.

This volume follows the same format as the first, with three excellent short introductions by Miller contextualizing Lacan's early seminar and his philosophical orientation. These are followed by Colette Soler's clear and concise essays on the symbolic, transference and interpretation. The volume also contains essays on the imaginary and the real as well as the Oedipus complex, the subject and Other, and Lacan's debt to Lévi-Strauss. There is a section on clinical perspectives, which addresses issues such as hysteria, obsessionality, transsexualism, fetishism and perversion. The cultural implications of Lacanian ideas are only peripherally touched upon in this volume in Marie Jaanus's 'A Civilization of Hatred', Fink's contribution on logical time,

Vincente Palomera's paper on ethics, and Žižek's discussion of Hegel and Lacan. *Reading Seminars I and II* concludes with the first English translation of Lacan's paper on the Freudian drive and the analyst's desire accompanied by a commentary by Miller.

Barnard, S. and Fink, B. (eds) (2002) *Reading Seminar XX: Lacan's Major Work on Love, Knowledge, and Feminine Sexuality*, Albany, New York: SUNY Press.

This is the most recent in the series and slightly different from the two preceding volumes, as there is no introduction by Miller and no new translation of a paper by Lacan. We do, however, find the familiar names of Soler on 'Hysteria in Scientific Discourse' and sexual difference; Fink on 'Knowledge and Jouissance'; and Žižek on 'The Real of Sexual Difference'; as well as Renata Salecl on 'Love Anxieties' and a paper by Paul Verhaeghe on 'Lacan's Answer to the Classical Mind/Body Deadlock'. Perhaps as a reflection of the brevity of Lacan's seminar *Encore*, this volume contains only nine contributions, and a couple of those are extremely short, but with Susanne Barnard's excellent introduction it does provide essential reading for anyone trying to understand this elusive and cryptic late seminar of Lacan.

INTRODUCTIONS TO LACAN

Over the last 20 years there have been numerous introductions to Lacan from various perspectives, disciplines and sympathies. I will indicate here just those non-clinical introductions I have found most helpful in understanding Lacan. For an extensive bibliography of works on Lacan see Michael Clark (1998) *Jacques Lacan: An Annotated Bibliography*, New York: Garland, 2 vols.

Benvenuto, B. and Kennedy, R. (1986) *The Works of Jacques Lacan: An Introduction*, New York: St Martin's Press.

This is rather an old introduction now, but as a chapter-by-chapter introduction to the English selection of the *Écrits* it is still useful and it has weathered better than most introductions from the 1980s. It is very clear and accessible and, as analysts, the authors were never tempted to reduce everything in Lacan to language. It also has a concluding chapter on *Encore*. If you have not read anything on Lacan before, this is as good a place to start as any and better than most.

Evans, D. (1996) *An Introductory Dictionary of Lacanian Psychoanalysis*, London: Routledge.

Evans gives us more than a simple dictionary here by contextualizing and tracing the various twists and turns of Lacan's major concepts. This is an essential work of reference for anyone studying Lacan.

Fink, B. (1995) *The Lacanian Subject: Between Language and Jouissance*, Princeton, NJ: Princeton University Press.

Fink's introduction is by no means easy reading, but it is by far the best introduction to Lacan currently available. The book is divided into four parts and considers Lacan's understanding of structure, subject, object and psychoanalysis as a discourse.

Nobus, D. (1998) *Key Concepts of Lacanian Psychoanalysis*, London: Rebus Press.

This collection contains the usual suspects, such as Fink on Lacan's four discourses and Žižek on fantasy. It has some very accessible chapters including Verhaeghe on the Lacanian subject, Nobus on the mirror phase, and Luke Thurston on Lacan's late and slightly insane ideas around the borromean knot, as well as Dylan Evans on Lacanian ethics, Russell Grigg on foreclosure and Katrien Libbrecht on desire and the analyst. Each contribution traces the development of these central concepts from early to late Lacan.

Roudinesco, E. (1993) *Jacques Lacan: Esquisse d'une vie, histoire d'un système des pensée*, Paris: Librairie Arthème Fayard (English version, *Jacques Lacan: An Outline of a Life and a History of a System of Thought*, trans. B. Bray, Cambridge: Polity Press, 1999).

This is essentially a more reader-friendly version of the second volume of Roudinesco's monumental three-volume history of psychoanalysis in France. Roudinesco thinks Lacan was a genius but at the same time narcissistic, authoritarian and ruthlessly ambitious. As an academic and trained psychoanalyst Roudinesco moves with ease from explicating complex psychoanalytic ideas to explaining Lacan's equally complex private life. At 500 pages the book seems rather daunting, but it reads fluently and the extensive appendices containing a wealth of information on the history of Lacan's publications, the various psychoanalytic associations etc. are extremely helpful. The orthodox Lacanians hate it.

LACAN AND CULTURAL THEORY

Adams, P. (1996) *The Emptiness of the Image: Psychoanalysis and Sexual Differences*, London: Routledge.

This collection of essays presents a sustained argument for the use of psychoanalysis in the analysis of culture, as well as a Lacanian understanding of sexual difference against feminist critiques. With brevity and clarity Adams deploys the Lacanian concepts of the *objet a* and the real to analyse the work of the artist Mary Kelly, performance artist Orlan, painter Francis Bacon, Michael Powell's film *Peeping Tom* (1960) and the representation of 'alternative' sexualities by Della Grace. Adams's work is by no means introductory, but it is exemplary of how Lacanian psychoanalysis can be used in the critique of representation.

Brooks, P. (1992) *Reading for the Plot: Design and Intention in Narrative*, Cambridge, MA: Harvard University Press.

This volume contains Brooks's classic essay 'Freud's Masterplot: A Model for Narrative'. Brooks takes Freud's 'Beyond the Pleasure Principle' as a model of narrative construction to develop a dynamic model of reader/text relations or what he calls an 'erotics of the text'. Brooks then deploys this model in readings of Stendhal, Dickens, Flaubert, Conrad and Faulkner. Brooks also reads Freud's case study of 'The Wolf Man' as an exemplary piece of modernist writing.

Copjec, J. (1994) *Read My Desire: Lacan Against the Historicists*, Cambridge, MA: MIT Press.

In this impressive but at times quite difficult collection of essays Copjec provides a sustained critique of Michel Foucault's notions of discourse and historicism. The volume contains many of Copjec's most well-known essays, including 'The Orthopsychic Subject: Film Theory and the Reception of Lacan', which challenges the conception of the subject adopted by film theory, and 'Sex and the Euthanasia of Reason', where she critiques Judith Butler's reading of Lacan and the discursive constitution of sex.

Cowie, E. (1997) *Representing the Woman: Cinema and Psychoanalysis*, London: Macmillan.

At 400 pages of densely written text Cowie's book is not an easy introduction to Lacanian film theory, but Cowie has been working in this area since its inception and this volume brings together her work over three decades. As such it addresses the central arguments of psychoanalytic film theory from the apparatus theorists of the 1970s through to the current debates on fantasy, the *objet a* and the real. Cowie always roots Lacanian ideas back in Freud and at the same time gives examples of specific film analysis. This is not a book one will sit down and read in one go, but it is essential to understand the development of psychoanalytic film theory.

Derrida, J. (1987) *The Post Card: From Socrates to Freud and Beyond*, trans. A. Bass, Chicago, IL: University of Chicago Press.

Derrida's reading of Freud's 'Beyond the Pleasure Principle' is an absolute tour de force; it is quite simply a brilliant piece of textual analysis. This volume also contains Derrida's most sustained engagement with Lacan, 'The Purveyor of Truth', where he reveals that what is at stake in the Poe seminar is actually the meaning of the phallus and the riddle of feminine sexuality. This is Derrida at his best.

Grosz, E. (1990) *Jacques Lacan: A Feminist Introduction*, London: Routledge.

For many years Grosz's text has provided the standard introduction to Lacan's theory of sexual difference. Orthodox Lacanians often hold it responsible for the misreading of Lacan in the Anglo-American academy. It is clear and accessible and you can make your own mind up.

Muller, J.P. and Richardson, W.J. (eds) (1988) *The Purloined Poe: Lacan, Derrida, and Psychoanalytic Reading*, Baltimore, MD: Johns Hopkins University Press.

This fascinating collection of essays brings together an exchange between the two giants of Post-structuralist theory, Lacan and Jacques Derrida. The volume opens with Poe's short story *The Purloined Letter*, Lacan's seminar on Poe and then Derrida's critique of Lacan. The volume also contains, however, a wealth of related material that has been generated by this exchange and in particular Barbara Johnson's brilliant assessment 'The Frame of Reference: Poe, Lacan, Derrida'. This collection is an essential starting point to understand the complex relationship between Lacanian psychoanalysis and Derridean 'deconstruction'.

Parkin-Gounelas, R. (2001) *Psychoanalysis and Literature: Intertextual Readings*, London: Palgrave.

Parkin-Gounelas's book is not strictly Lacanian, but it has the advantage over many texts in the area of being based on literary examples.

Parkin-Gounelas explores concepts such as the mirror stage, the symbolic, abjection, hysteria, masquerade, the *objet a* and the death drive from authors as diverse as John Milton, George Eliot, Virginia Woolf, Bram Stoker and Sylvia Plath. This is an excellent introduction in how to read psychoanalytically.

Rabaté, J.-M. (2001) *Jacques Lacan*, London: Palgrave.

Rabaté does not set out to offer us Lacanian readings of texts, but rather to establish Lacan's theory of literature. Rabaté explores Lacan's reading of specific authors from Shakespeare, through Poe, André Gide and the Marquis de Sade to James Joyce, as well as his writing on tragedy and courtly love. This is an extremely useful guide to Lacan's reading of literature and has a good annotated bibliography at the end.

Rose, J. (1996) *Sexuality in the Field of Vision*, London: Verso.

The essays collected in this volume may now seem dated, but many of the interventions between psychoanalysis, feminism and politics contained here are landmark texts. Rose is always sharp and insightful and these texts are essential reading if one wants to understand how a certain kind of feminist psychoanalytic politics developed.

Vice, S. (ed.) (1996) *Psychoanalytic Criticism: A Reader*, Cambridge: Polity Press.

This useful collection of essays contains extracts from psychoanalysts as well as from some of the most important works of contemporary psychoanalytic criticism. Peter Nicholls offers an exemplary reading of Toni Morrison's *Beloved* in terms of Freud's 'nachträglichkeit' or 'deferred action'. Vice also provides helpful contextualizing introductions to each selection of extracts.

Wright, E. (1999) *Speaking Desires Can Be Dangerous: The Poetics of the Unconscious*, Cambridge: Polity Press.

This book differs from other works of psychoanalytic criticism in that Wright engages with both literary and clinical texts. As a trained analyst, Wright reads literature and film – Shakespeare, Robert Coover, Kiéslowski – with a clinical eye and, as a literary critic, she reads clinical material – Freud, Lacan, Kristeva, Bion – with a literary one. The chapter 'What is a Discourse?' provides as good an introduction to Lacan's idea of discourse as you are likely to find.

Žižek, S. (1992) *Looking Awry: An Introduction to Jacques Lacan Through Popular Culture*, Cambridge, MA: MIT Press.

Of Žižek's many books (at least two a year) it is difficult to choose one. *The Sublime Object of Ideology* (1989) contains most of his ideas full-blown and *Tarrying with the Negative* (1993) offers a sustained reflection on his philosophical, political and psychoanalytic background, but *Looking Awry* is unquestionably his most popular and most accessibly written work. The first section provides a remarkably clear and lucid account of Lacanian concepts such as fantasy, the *objet a* and the real. Part II sets out a wonderful Lacanian analysis of Hitchcock and Part III offers a critique of postmodernity. This is a very entertaining introduction to Lacan and will probably make you a Žižek fan for life.

Žižek, S. (2001) *The Fright of Real Tears: Krzysztof Kiéslowski Between Theory and Post-Theory*, London, BFI Publishing.

In this volume Žižek mounts a passionate defence of Lacanian film theory, as practised by Joan Copjec and himself, and heavily criticized from within the discipline of film studies. Žižek persuasively shows how many of the criticisms of Lacanian film studies are based on a serious misrepresentation of Lacanian ideas and then offers us a reading of the Polish director Kiéslowski, among others. This will not persuade his critics in film departments, but it clarifies a number of key concepts such as 'suture' and the 'sinthome'.

WEBSITE

http://www.lacan.com

The online journal *lacanian ink* provides some of the most interesting and up-to-date work in contemporary Lacanian studies.

WORKS CITED

WORKS BY JACQUES LACAN

—— (1938) 'La famille', in *Encyclopédie française*, Paris: Larousse.

—— (1975 [1932]) *De la psychose paranoïaque dans ses rapports avec la personnalité*, Paris: Seuil.

—— (1977a [1949]) 'The Mirror Stage as Formative of the Function of the I as Revealed in Psychoanalytic Experience', in *Écrits: A Selection*, trans. A. Sheridan, London: Routledge/Tavistock, pp. 1–7.

—— (1977b [1956]) 'The Function and Field of Speech and Language in Psychoanalysis', in *Écrits: A Selection*, trans. A. Sheridan, London: Routledge/Tavistock, pp. 30–113.

—— (1977c [1957]) 'The Agency of the Letter in the Unconscious or Reason Since Freud', in *Écrits: A Selection*, trans. A. Sheridan, London: Routledge/Tavistock, pp. 146–78.

—— (1977d [1958]) 'The Signification of the Phallus', in *Écrits: A Selection*, trans. A. Sheridan, London: Routledge/Tavistock, pp. 281–91.

—— (1977e [1960]) 'The Subversion of the Subject and the Dialectic of Desire in the Freudian Unconscious', in *Écrits: A Selection*, trans. A. Sheridan, London: Routledge/Tavistock, pp. 292–325.

—— (1979 [1973]) *The Seminar of Jacques Lacan, Book XI: The Four Fundamental Concepts of Psychoanalysis 1964–1965*, ed. J.-A. Miller, trans. A. Sheridan, Harmondsworth: Penguin.

—— (1982 [1959]) 'Desire and the Interpretation of Desire in *Hamlet*', trans. J. Hulbert, in S. Felman (ed.) *Literature and Psychoanalysis, The Question of Reading: Otherwise*, Baltimore, MD: The Johns Hopkins University Press, pp. 11–52.

—— (1988a [1975]) *The Seminar of Jacques Lacan, Book I: Freud's Papers on Technique 1953–1954*, ed. J.-A. Miller, trans. J. Forrester, Cambridge: Cambridge University Press.

—— (1988b [1978]) *The Seminar of Jacques Lacan, Book II: The Ego in Freud's Theory and in the Technique of Psychoanalysis 1954–1955*, ed. J.-A. Miller, trans. S. Tomaselli, Cambridge: Cambridge University Press.

—— (1988c [1956]) 'Seminar on *The Purloined Letter*', trans. J. Mehlman, in J.P. Muller and W.J. Richardson (eds) *The Purloined Poe: Lacan, Derrida and Psychoanalytic Reading*, Baltimore, MD: The Johns Hopkins University Press, pp. 28–54.

—— (1990 [1974]) *Television: A Challenge to the Psychoanalytic Establishment*, ed. J. Copjec, trans. D. Hollier, R. Krauss, A. Michelson and J. Mehlman, New York: Norton.

—— (1992 [1986]) *The Seminar of Jacques Lacan, Book VII: The Ethics of Psychoanalysis 1959–1960*, ed. J.-A. Miller, trans. D. Porter, London: Routledge.

—— (1993 [1981]) *The Seminar of Jacques Lacan, Book III: The Psychoses 1955–1956*, ed. J.-A. Miller, trans. R. Grigg, London: Routledge.

—— (1995 [1964]) 'Position of the Unconscious', trans. B. Fink, in R. Feldstein, B. Fink and M. Jaanus (eds) *Reading Seminar XI: Lacan's Four Fundamental Concepts of Psychoanalysis*, New York: SUNY Press, pp. 259–82.

—— (1998 [1975]) *The Seminar of Jacques Lacan, Book XX: Encore, On Feminine Sexuality, The Limits of Love and Knowledge 1972–1973*, ed. J.-A. Miller, trans. B. Fink, New York: Norton.

SECONDARY TEXTS

Adams, P. (1996a) 'Operation Orlan', in *The Emptiness of the Image: Psychoanalysis and Sexual Differences*, London: Routledge, pp. 141–59.

—— (1996b) 'Waiving the Phallus', in *The Emptiness of the Image: Psychoanalysis and Sexual Differences*, London: Routledge, pp. 49–56.

Adams, P. and Cowie, E. (eds) (1990) *The Woman in Question*, London: Verso.

Althusser, L. (1984a [1964]) 'Freud and Lacan', in *Essays on Ideology*, London: Verso, pp. 141–71.

—— (1984b [1971]) 'Ideology and Ideological State Apparatuses (Notes Towards an Investigation)', in *Essays on Ideology*, London: Verso, pp. 1–60.

Appignanesi, L. and Forrester, J. (1993) *Freud's Women*, London: Virago.

Badiou, A. (2002) *Ethics: An Essay on the Understanding of Evil*, trans. P. Hallward, London: Verso.

Barnard, S. and Fink, B. (eds) (2002) *Reading Seminar XX: Lacan's Major Work on Love, Knowledge, and Feminine Sexuality*, Albany, NY: SUNY Press.

Barthes, R. (1977a [1966]) 'Introduction to the Structural Analysis of Narrative', in *Image, Music, Text*, trans. S. Heath, London: Fontana Press, pp. 79–124.

—— (1977b [1968]) 'The Death of the Author', in *Image, Music, Text*, trans. S. Heath, London: Fontana Press, pp. 142–8.

—— (1984 [1980]) *Camera Lucida*, London: Flamingo.

—— (1985 [1967]) *The Fashion System*, trans. M. Ward and R. Howard, New York: Hill and Wang.

—— (1990 [1973]) *The Pleasure of the Text*, trans. R. Miller, Oxford: Basil Blackwell.

Baudry, J.-L. (1974–5) 'Ideological Effects of the Basic Cinematographic Apparatus', trans. A. Williams, *Film Quarterly*, 28 (2): 39–47.

Benvenuto, B. and Kennedy, R. (1986) *The Works of Jacques Lacan: An Introduction*, New York: St Martins Press.

Bhabha, H.K. (1994) *The Location of Culture*, London: Routledge.

Brennan, T. (ed.) (1989) *Between Feminism and Psychoanalysis*, London: Routledge.

Brooks, P. (1987) 'The Idea of a Psychoanalytic Literary Criticism', in S. Rimmon-Kenan (ed.) *Discourse in Psychoanalysis and Literature*, London: Methuen, pp. 1–18.

—— (1992) *Reading for the Plot: Design and Intention in Narrative*, Cambridge, MA: Harvard University Press.

Burgin, V. (1986) 'Re-reading *Camera Lucida*', in *The End of Art Theory: Criticism And Postmodernity*, London: Macmillan, pp. 71–92.

Butler, J. (1993) *Bodies That Matter: On the Discursive Limits of Sex*, London: Routledge.

Castoriadis, C. (1987) *The Imaginary Constitution of Society*, trans. K. Blamey, Cambridge: Polity Press.

Clark, M. (1998) *Jacques Lacan: An Annotated Bibliography*, 2 vols, New York: Garland.

Copjec, J. (1994a) 'Sex and the Euthanasia of Reason', in *Read My Desire: Lacan Against the Historicists*, Cambridge, MA: MIT Press, pp. 201–36.

—— (1994b) 'The Orthopsychic Subject: Film Theory and the Reception of Lacan', in *Read My Desire: Lacan Against the Historicists*, Cambridge, MA: MIT Press, pp. 15–38.

Cowie, E. (1990) 'Fantasia', in P. Adams and E. Cowie (eds) *The Woman in Question*, London: Verso, pp. 149–96.

—— (1997) *Representing the Woman: Cinema and Psychoanalysis*, London: Macmillan.

Derrida, J. (1987) *The Post Card: From Socrates to Freud and Beyond*, trans. A. Bass, Chicago, IL: University of Chicago Press.

Descartes, R. (1968 [1642]) *Discourse on Method and the Mediations*, trans. F.E. Sutcliffe, Harmondsworth: Penguin.

Eagleton, T. (1983) *Literary Theory: An Introduction*, Oxford: Basil Blackwell.

Elliott, A. (1998) *Social Theory and Psychoanalysis in Transition: Self and Society from Freud to Kristeva*, Oxford: Basil Blackwell.

Evans, D. (1996) *An Introductory Dictionary of Lacanian Psychoanalysis*, London: Routledge.

Feldstein, R., Fink, B. and Jaanus, M. (eds) (1995) *Reading Seminar XI: Lacan's Four Fundamental Concepts of Psychoanalysis*, New York: SUNY Press.

——, —— and —— (1996) *Reading Seminars I and II: Lacan's Return to Freud*, New York: SUNY Press.

Feldstein, R., Fink, B. and Jaanus, M. (eds)

Felman, S. (ed.) (1982) *Literature and Psychoanalysis, The Question of Reading: Otherwise*, Cambridge, MA: Harvard University Press.

Fink, B. (1995) *The Lacanian Subject: Between Language and Jouissance*, Princeton, NJ: Princeton University Press.

—— (2002) 'Knowledge and Jouissance', in S. Barnard and B. Fink (eds) *Reading Seminar XX: Lacan's Major Work on Love, Knowledge, and Feminine Sexuality*, New York: SUNY Press, pp. 21–45.

Freud, S. (1954 [1895]) 'Project for a Scientific Psychology', reprinted in *The Standard Edition of the Complete Psychological Works of Sigmund Freud*, vol. I, trans. James Strachey, London: Hogarth Press and Institute of Psychoanalysis, pp. 281–392.

—— (1984a [1923]) *The Ego and the Id*, in *On Metapsychology: The Theory of Psychoanalysis*, Penguin Freud Library, vol. 11, Harmondsworth: Penguin, pp. 339–408.

—— (1984b [1920]) *Beyond the Pleasure Principle*, in *On Metapsychology: The Theory of Psychoanalysis*, Penguin Freud Library, vol. 11, Harmondsworth: Penguin, pp. 269–338.

—— (1984c [1915]) 'Instincts and Their Vicissitudes', in *On Metapsychology: The Theory of Psychoanalysis*, Penguin Freud Library, vol. 11, Harmondsworth: Penguin, pp. 105–38.

—— (1984d [1917]) 'Mourning and Melancholia', in *On Metapsychology: The Theory of Psychoanalysis*, Penguin Freud Library, vol. 11, Harmondsworth: Penguin, pp. 245–68.

—— (1991a [1900]) *The Interpretation of Dreams*, Penguin Freud Library, vol. 4, Harmondsworth: Penguin.

—— (1991b [1901]) *The Psychopathology of Everyday Life*, Penguin Freud Library, vol. 5, Harmondsworth: Penguin.

—— (1991c [1905]) *Jokes and Their Relation to the Unconscious*, Penguin Freud Library, vol. 6, Harmondsworth: Penguin.

—— (1991d [1905]) *Three Essays on the Theory of Sexuality*, in *On Sexuality*, Penguin Freud Library, vol. 7, Harmondsworth: Penguin, pp. 31–169.

—— (1991e [1923]) 'The Infantile Genital Organization (An Interpolation into the Theory of Sexuality)', in *On Sexuality*, Penguin Freud Library, vol. 7, Harmondsworth: Penguin, pp. 303–12.

—— (1991f [1930]) *Civilization and Its Discontents*, in *Civilization, Society and Religion*, Penguin Freud Library, vol. 12, Harmondsworth: Penguin, pp. 243–340.

—— (1991g [1913]) *Totem and Taboo*, in *The Origins of Religion*, Penguin Freud Library, vol. 13, Harmondsworth: Penguin, pp. 43–224.

Grosz, E. (1990) *Jacques Lacan: A Feminist Introduction*, London: Routledge.

Heath, S. (1986) 'Joan Riviere and the Masquerade', in V. Burgin, J. Donald and C. Kaplan (eds) *Formations of Fantasy*, London: Routledge, pp. 45–61.

Irigaray, L (1985a [1974]) *Speculum of the Other Woman*, trans. C. Porter, Ithaca, NY: Cornell University Press.

—— (1985b [1977]) *This Sex Which is Not One*, trans. C. Porter, Ithaca, NY: Cornell University Press.

—— (1991) 'The Poverty of Psychoanalysis', in M. Whitford (ed.) *The Irigaray Reader*, Oxford: Blackwell, pp. 79–104.

Iversen, M. (1994) 'What is a Photograph?', *Art History*, 17 (3): 450–63.

Jones, E. (1927) 'Early Development of Female Sexuality', *International Journal of Psycho-Analysis*, 8: 459–72.

—— (1949) *Hamlet and Oedipus*, London: Victor Gollancz.

Kristeva, J. (1984 [1974]) *Revolution in Poetic Language*, trans. L.S. Roudiez, New York: Columbia University Press.

Laclau, E. (1990) *New Reflections on the Revolution of Our Time*, London: Verso.

Laclau, E. and Mouffe, C. (1985) *Hegemony and Socialist Strategy: Towards a Radical Democratic Politics*, London: Verso.

Laplanche, J. and Leclaire, S. (1972 [1965]) 'The Unconscious: A Psychoanalytic Study', *Yale French Studies*, 48: 118–78.

Laplanche, J. and Pontalis, J.-B. (1986 [1968]) 'Fantasy and the Origins of Sexuality', in V. Burgin, J. Donald and C. Kaplan (eds) *Formations of Fantasy*, London: Routledge.

Lévi-Strauss, C. (1966) 'The Culinary Triangle' in *New Society*, December 22 (221): 937–40.

—— (1969 [1949]) 'The Elementary Structures of Kinship', trans. J.H. Bell and J.R. von Sturmer, Boston, MA: Deacon Press.

McGowan, T. and Kunkle, S. (eds) (2004) *Lacan and Contemporary Film*, New York: The Other Press.

Metz, C. (1982) *Psychoanalysis and Cinema: The Imaginary Signifier*, London: Macmillan.

Miller, J.-A. (1996) 'An Introduction to Seminars I and II', in R. Feldstein, B. Fink and M. Jaanus (eds) *Reading Seminars I and II: Lacan's Return to Freud*, New York: SUNY Press, pp. 3–35.

Millet, K. (1977 [1969]) *Sexual Politics*, London: Virago.

Mitchell, J. and Rose, J. (eds) (1982) *Feminine Sexuality: Jacques Lacan and the École Freudienne*, London: Routledge.

Moi, T. (1985) *Sexual/Textual Politics: Feminist Literary Theory*, London: Routledge.

Mouffe, C. (1990) 'The Legacy of m/f', in P. Adams and E. Cowie (eds) *The Woman in Question*, London: Verso, pp. 3–5.

—— (1993) *The Return of the Political*, London: Verso.

Muller, J.P. and Richarson, W.J. (eds) (1988) *The Purloined Poe: Lacan, Derrida and Psychoanalytic Reading*, Baltimore, MD: Johns Hopkins University Press.

Mulvey, L. (1975) 'Visual Pleasure and Narrative Cinema', *Screen*, 16 (3): 6–18.

Nobus, D. (1998) 'Life and Death in the Glass: A New Look at the Mirror Stage', in D. Nobus (ed.) *Key Concepts of Lacanian Psychoanalysis*, London: Rebus Press, pp. 101–38.

Parkin-Gounelas, R. (2001) *Psychoanalysis and Literature: Intertextual Readings*, London: Palgrave.

Penley, C. (1989) 'Feminism, Film Theory, and Bachelor Machines', in *The Future of an Illusion: Film, Feminism and Psychoanalysis*, London: Routledge.

Rabaté, J.-M. (2001) *Jacques Lacan*, London, Palgrave.

Ragland-Sullivan, E. (1995) *Essays on the Pleasures of Death: From Freud to Lacan*, London: Routledge.

Riviere, J. (1986 [1929]) 'Womanliness as a Masquerade', in V. Burgin, J. Donald and C. Kaplan (eds) *Formations of Fantasy*, London: Routledge, pp. 35–44.

Rose, J. (1996a) 'Feminine Sexuality: Jacques Lacan and the *École Freudienne*', in *Sexuality in the Field of Vision*, London: Verso, pp. 49–81.

—— (1996b) 'The Cinematic Apparatus: Problems in Current Theory', in *Sexuality in the Field of Vision*, London: Verso, pp. 199–213.

—— (1996c) 'Femininity and its Discontents', in *Sexuality in the Field of Vision*, London: Verso, pp. 83–103.

Roudinesco, E. (1999) *Jacques Lacan: An Outline of a Life and a History of a System of Thought*, trans. B. Bray, Cambridge: Polity Press.

Salecl, R. (2002) 'Love Anxieties', in S. Barnard and B. Fink (eds) *Reading Seminar XX: Lacan's Major Work on Love, Knowledge, and Feminine Sexuality*, New York: SUNY Press, pp. 93–98.

Salecl, R. and Žižek, S. (eds) (1996) *Gaze and Voice as Love Objects*, Durham: Duke University Press.

Sartre, J.-P. (1972) *Transcendence of the Ego: An Existentialist Theory of Consciousness*, New York, Octagon Books.

Saussure, F. de (1983 [1916]) *Course in General Linguistics*, trans. R. Harris, La Salle, IL: Open Court.

Soler, C. (1995a) 'The Subject and the Other (II)', in R. Feldstein, B. Fink and M. Jaanus (eds) *Reading Seminar XI: Lacan's Four Fundamental Concepts of Psychoanalysis*, New York: SUNY Press, pp. 45–53.

—— (1995b) 'The Body in the Teaching of Jacques Lacan', *Journal of the Centre for Freudian Analysis and Research*, 6: 6–38.

—— (2002) 'What Does the Unconscious Know about Women?', in S. Barnard and B. Fink (eds) *Reading Seminar XX: Lacan's Major Work on Love, Knowledge, and Feminine Sexuality*, New York: SUNY Press, pp. 99–108.

Stavrakakis, Y. (1999) *Lacan and the Political*, London: Routledge.

Tallis, R. (1997) 'The Shrink from Hell', *The Times Higher Education Supplement*, October 31: 20.

Thurschwell, P. (2000) *Sigmund Freud*, Routledge Critical Thinkers, London: Routledge.

Turkle, S. (1992) *Psychoanalytic Politics: Jacques Lacan and Freud's French Revolution*, 2nd edn, London: Free Association Books.

Verhaeghe, P. (1998) 'Causation and Destitution of a Pre-ontological Non-entity: On The Lacanian Subject', in D. Nobus (ed.) *Key Concepts of Lacanian Psychoanalysis*, London: Rebus Press, pp. 164–89.

Vice, S. (ed.) (1996) *Psychoanalytic Criticism: A Reader*, Cambridge: Polity Press.

Whitford, M. (1991) *Luce Irigaray: Philosophy in the Feminine*, London: Routledge.

Wilson, Edmund (1965) 'The Ambiguity of Henry James', in *The Triple Thinkers*, Harmondsworth: Penguin.

Wright, E. (1998) *Psychoanalytic Criticism: A Reappraisal*, 2nd edn, Cambridge: Polity Press.

—— (1999) *Speaking Desires Can Be Dangerous: The Poetics of the Unconscious*, Cambridge: Polity Press.

Žižek, S. (1989) *The Sublime Object of Ideology*, London: Verso.

—— (1992) *Looking Awry: An Introduction to Jacques Lacan Through Popular Culture*, Cambridge, MA: The MIT Press.

—— (1993) *Tarrying With the Negative: Kant, Hegel, and the Critique of Ideology*, Durham: Duke University Press.

—— (1994) *The Metastases of Enjoyment: Six Essays on Woman and Causality*, London: Verso.

—— (2001) *The Fright of Real Tears: Krzysztof Kiéslowski Between Theory and Post-theory*, London: BFI Publishing.

INDEX

Écrits: A Selection
Jacques Lacan

'Lacan's work marks a crucial moment in the history of psychoanalysis, a moment which will perhaps prove as significant as Freud's original discovery of the unconscious.'

Colin McCabe

Écrits: A Selection is Lacan's most important work, bringing together 27 articles and lectures originally published between 1936 and 1966. To this day, Lacan's radical, brilliant and complex ideas continue to be highly influential in everything from film theory to art history and literary criticism. *Écrits: A Selection* is the essential source for anyone who seeks to understand this seminal thinker and his influence on contemporary thought and culture.

Hb: 0–415–25546–5   Pb: 0–415–25392–6